Out of the Rabbit Hole
Breaking the Cycle of Addiction

Out of the Rabbit Hole
Breaking the Cycle of Addiction

Evidence-Based Treatment for Adolescents
with Co-occurring Disorders

Deborah A. Berberich, PhD

To order additional copies of this book, contact:
Xlibris Corporation
1-888-795-4274
www.Xlibris.com
Orders@Xlibris.com
126068

Contents

PART FIVE—The Bridge

PART SIX—Evolution

PART SEVEN—Personal Genesis

Dedicated to John G. Berberich V

A Free and Loving Spirit

Many young people who struggle with drug addiction also struggle with psychological issues or mental illness such as bipolar disorder, major depressive disorder, and anxiety, obsessive, or thought disorders. A significant part of their struggle is the stigma attached to both disorders and the reluctance of too many health care providers to see them as individuals, as opposed to merely "addicts." Although research has clearly demonstrated that both addiction and mental illness need to be treated simultaneously, most treatment programs in the community focus primarily on one disorder or the other.

This book recognizes the particularly challenging needs of adolescents suffering from co-occurring disorders and is formulated on evidence-based treatment recommendations. The purpose is to help adolescents and their families better understand substance abuse and mental disorders and how to get the help they need as well as to encourage clinicians and drug counselors to develop a more integrated and coordinated system of care. The final goal of this book is to help young people who are currently struggling with addiction achieve sobriety, stability, and a newfound sense of purpose and hope for their future.

I would like to offer a special acknowledgment to my son Adam, for all his legal and literary feedback and contribution to this book.

Preface

HOPE

The primary purpose of this book is to help people understand addiction and the dynamic role between addiction and mental illness. Addiction complicates mental illness by increasing and prolonging psychiatric symptoms. Relapse is not an indication of individual failure but rather an indication that treatment failed to address the specific needs of that individual. The first step to recovery is knowledge.

This book describes the basic components of addiction, treatment, and the recovery process. It is the ambition of this book to increase understanding and access to care and to instill an unwavering belief that with the appropriate treatment and continued support, there is absolute and undisputed hope for achieving sustained recovery from addiction.

"Nicotine, alcohol, ecstasy, cocaine, heroin . . . every substance leaves a unique trail of devastation as unmistakable as a fingerprint" (Steven Karch, pathologist, quoted in Bokelmann 2011, 71). Drug abuse is a systemic problem impacting more than the individual who is abusing substances; it affects their family, friends, local community, and society as a whole. The total economic cost of drug abuse in the United States has been estimated to be close to 215 billion dollars.

One study reported that in 2006, over 38,390 people died as a result of drugs in the United States (Heron et al. 2009). In 2007, there were 12.1 deaths per million people in the United States alone directly attributed to drug abuse (United States Department of Justice, National Drug Intelligence Center 2010). In 2010, the population in the United States was 308,745,538 (United States Census Bureau 2010), and with over 300 million people in the United States, given the 2007 statistic of 12.1 deaths per million people—seemingly unimpressive in itself—*this could easily translate to over twenty-five million drug-abuse-related deaths per year.* Substance abuse is thus a problem of national concern.

Many of the ideas presented in this book are not derived from Mars, but from clinical and personal experience as well as research compiled by professionals and organizations dedicated to improving treatment success for addiction recovery. A special acknowledgment goes to the United States Department of Health and Human Services, Substance Abuse and Mental Health Services Administration, National Institute on Drug Abuse, and the National Institute of Mental Health for all their combined efforts and contributions in the area of co-occurring disorders.

People who become addicted do not do so by premeditation or design. Many start out during adolescence through innocent (naive) experimentation, usually by simply trying to fit in with their peers, and are fooled by the immediate and short-lived effects of the drug into believing that using helps them to feel better. In short, individuals who struggle for the majority of their life with their personal demons of addiction do not start using drugs in a vacuum; there are multiple biological, psychological, and social factors involved.

Too many people have found their battle with addiction far too powerful to conquer by themselves, and unfortunately, far too many give up trying to achieve recovery. To add to the difficulty of an uphill battle, when it comes to addressing co-occurring disorders, there is a shocking lack of community-based health care support available, especially for adolescents.

Despite a wealth of research that clearly demonstrates the need to combine treatments addressing addiction and mental illness, there seems to be a void in the real world of available treatments, especially for adolescents who come from low- to middle-income families. Even in rare cases when a family does have insurance, it typically only pays for detoxification or other short-term, crisis-oriented care; it fails to pay for necessary and effective long-term treatment, and most families do not have the resources to pay out of pocket for any extended care.

We have all passed by the disheveled youth standing outside a store, asking for some change. Too often are there young and not-so-young people sleeping outside on the ground or on benches. Having spent a fair amount of time talking with many of these self-deceptive and tortured souls, I can tell you that quite a few surprisingly came from "good" homes with loving parents. For one reason or another, they ran away from home or were kicked out by their parents who just couldn't continue to cope with the thefts, the lying, and the frustrations of having a child who had, in many ways, become a stranger. Most parents are overwhelmed and unable to deal with the inherent pain related to having a child who suffers from drug abuse.

Combating drug abuse is far more complicated than simply attempting to teach our children to "just say no" (Elliott 1993), and turning our backs to them once that fails is not the answer. This only creates a complexity of problems and costs for all as well as an invaluable loss of human potential and the shattering of many youthful dreams. As a society, we should never give up on our children. We need to help them save hope and know that no matter how dire things may seem, how seemingly hopeless and frustrating, it is always darkest before the dawn. Recovery is always possible.

Although some terminology used throughout this book may seem a bit academic, the words used are not to impress or confuse. It is important to be familiar with some of the complicated concepts in order to understand the basic causes of addiction and the fundamental roadblocks to recovery. I found in teaching these concepts to individuals who were incarcerated for drug-related crimes that an understanding of the neurological and biological components involved in addiction helped them reduce or even eliminate their need to use (yes, people have access to drugs in prison). After such an understanding, many have told me, "Now it all makes sense." By demystifying it, addiction lost its "magical hold" and much of its power over them. Sadly, however, despite best intentions, most people that have ended up in the prison system have been demoralized by their years of addiction and criminal lifestyle, have not developed basic life and job skills, have lost all or most social and family support, and therefore face tremendous difficulty maintaining recovery and hope. The solution therefore is to address the problem of addiction earlier, during adolescence, when the brain is still forming and before too much "collateral damage" has occurred.

This book addresses adolescents and young adults who struggle with substance abuse and the challenges of a variety of mental disorders. Despite the apparent negative stigma of the term "mental disorders," this term includes any teenager who struggles with depression, anxiety, and unstable moods, which can be just about anyone during these difficult times.

Someone who suffers with a psychological disorder, such as bipolar disorder or major depressive disorder, and a substance abuse disorder is referred to as having a co-occurring disorder. It is the hope of this author that individuals who are struggling with a co-occurring disorder, family members, friends, educators, law enforcement, and all other potential community support systems become familiar with the basic concepts put forth in this book. A better understanding of the factors and dynamics involved in addiction will enable our community to better support struggling individuals achieve recovery. No one should ever have to go through the battle for recovery alone.

PART ONE

A Generational Crisis

Past and Current Hurdles

Substance abuse and mental health disorders are now recognized as significant obstacles to adolescent development. Adolescence is an important and neurologically sensitive period of life, a time during which an unfortunate number of young people experiment with alcohol and drugs. This is also the developmental period of life in which mental illness can begin to surface. Among those who experiment for one "justification" or another, adolescents suffering from mental health disorders including depression, anxiety, and mood disorders have an increased risk for abusing substances in comparison to their peers. Often individuals report that they use drugs or alcohol to feel "normal"—less depressed or anxious. There is sadly some truth to this desire as the very same brain structures involved with addiction are involved with depression and anxiety.

Adolescence is an important developmental period during which the transition from childhood to adulthood is refined both physically and psychologically. During this period, the prefrontal lobes of the cerebral cortex involved in decision making, among other important functions, are still developing. Substance abuse throws a serious roadblock to this development. It interferes with the acquisition of important psychological and cognitive functions such as critical thinking, judgment, reality testing, and problem-solving skills. To sum this up, individuals who chronically use substances during adolescence disrupt the development of the mental skills and abilities necessary to effectively deal with what life throws at them. The problems may be temporary, but increasing reliance on substances can consume an individual so completely that they eventually find themselves at the bottom of a rabbit hole, believing there is no way out.

In the past fifty years, addiction has been widely researched. The National Institute on Drug Abuse (NIDA 2009, 2) describes addiction as a "complex but treatable disease that affects brain function and behavior." Some of the variables that factor into the development of addiction are genetics, biology, psychology, personality, and an adolescent's cultural-socioeconomic environment. These variables interact in an exponential fashion, and the whole is, in fact, far greater than the sum of its parts. Through an evaluation of research, NIDA has identified and defined important factors of a successful treatment program (NIDA 2009). Their research supports my personal experience and knowledge largely due to having worked with individuals who have had serious consequences in their lives from their personal demons (i.e., drugs of choice). The essence of the NIDA recommendation for effective treatment is the recognition that the process of addiction is multifarious.

Currently there is little assistance available to an adolescent who may be suffering from a mental illness combined with a substance abuse co-occurring disorder. The barriers to effective treatment are compounded with the financial inaccessibility of treatment, in that the range of cost for inpatient treatment of a co-occurring disorder can range as high as ninety thousand dollars per month. Most families do not make that level of income per year, and most insurance providers do not cover anything but short-term, crisis-oriented treatment.

Despite the involvement of multiple governmental agencies in the welfare of our youth, these agencies do not operate effectively as an integrated system (National Academy of Sciences 2009). An international awareness for the need to integrate mental health and medical health treatment resulted in a multiple agency conference to address this issue and to create the concept of "no wrong door" (COAG 2006; QLD 2007). Despite the call for a "no wrong door" policy, there are too few entry doors for coordinating treatment in place. Too many youth fall into the cracks between agencies and providers. Drug counselors are not typically trained to work with adolescents with a mental illness, and many mental health providers report feeling uncomfortable working with teenagers with a drug addiction (National Academy of Science 2009). Additionally, many teenagers do not want to admit to their addiction and are unlikely to openly discuss it with their therapist. Similarly, they are not willing to accept or discuss underlying mental health concerns they may have with their drug counselor and certainly not in sobriety-oriented group sessions (e.g., 12-step programs) with their peers.

Continuity of care means that different providers such as inpatient hospitals, outpatient therapists, psychiatrists, and drug counselors work together to allow a smooth transition between their services. Despite the awareness of the need for this transition and coordination between providers and the "no wrong door" policy, this concept has yet to take hold in the treatment of adolescents. Adolescent psychiatric facilities are typically set up for short-term crisis intervention and do not have adequate therapeutic assistance available for anything more than stabilization of an acute phase of a psychological disorder. Psychiatric facilities do not typically or adequately address drug addiction. If it is determined that a teenager suffers with a substance abuse disorder, mental health providers too quickly dismiss symptoms, writing them off as indicators of addiction and perhaps "drug-seeking behavior" and deny the adolescent effective treatment. If an adolescent has a substance abuse disorder, they are referred out to substance abuse providers. At best, they are afforded inpatient care only if they have insurance and are in need of medical detoxification. Outpatient treatment, on the other hand, is typically short-term, not usually integrated or evidence-based, and therefore insufficient to help the individual attain and maintain stability of their mental health symptoms and sobriety from their substance abuse disorder.

The travesty of our current system of care is the sad reality that for most families, when an adolescent has a co-occurring mental health and substance abuse disorder, they are unlikely to receive any semblance of treatment until they have fallen into the juvenile justice system. The juvenile arrest rate in the United States of youth between the ages of ten to seventeen had a sharp increase between the early to late 1990s. Although there has been a slight reduction in the current decade, at a rate of approximately 540 per 100,000 of adolescents incarcerated for drug-related charges, the numbers are still double to what they were in the 1980s. This clearly demonstrates that despite a modest statistical downturn, addiction is, in fact, a growing problem (SAMHSA 2011) and, arguably, a modern-day epidemic.

As stated earlier, too many of our youth with co-occurring disorders end up in the criminal justice system. A review of the most recently available statistics indicated that in the United States, there were 170,300 drug-abuse-related arrests of adolescents between the ages of twelve to seventeen (Office of Juvenile Justice and Delinquency Prevention 2009). In California, there were sixty thousand juvenile felony arrests in 2005, and drug offenses accounted for 10 percent of these arrests (California Legislative Analyst Department 2007). California has not been keeping records over the past several years due to budgetary reasons, but in 1995, the cost to incarcerate an adolescent was over thirty thousand dollars per year. Substance abuse disorders are a problem that impacts individuals and society as a whole, including those who may not be directly affected by drug addiction. There is a need for a better system to identify at-risk youth before they end up incarcerated for a drug-related charge and in the juvenile justice system. Not only would it save lives, it also would save countless dollars to put such a system in place.

Mental health professionals in the criminal justice system are, by necessity, generally more focused on violence and other criminal, behavioral issues than mental illness. Once in the criminal justice system, an individual has a whole new realm of concerns, including their personal safety. Many incarcerated individuals chose to ignore their mental health issues for a very real concern of being singled out by others as weak. Some ethnic and racial groups in prison strongly "discourage" members in their group from seeking mental health treatment and have no difficulty using violence to impose this rule.

Once an individual is incarcerated, they are essentially on their own. They are effectively forgotten by society, and it is typically a downward spiral as they become increasingly demoralized, marginalized, and criminalized.

Although there is extensive research regarding addiction and the many different approaches to treating addiction, the current relapse rate for addiction is too high. Addiction contributes to increased health problems, increased mortality, lower quality of life, criminal thinking, and an overall unacceptable loss of human potential. There is a lack of integration of research and understanding of addiction applied to the actual treatment of addiction. Further, as stated before, there is an overall lack of accessibility to treatment for adolescents from low- to middle-income families. More extensive, although not necessarily fully effective, treatment appears to be reserved for the wealthy.

Depending on many variables, including the drug of choice, a review of all available statistics indicates that the rate of relapse at best appears to be greater than 50 percent for a period of less than ninety days. Additionally, the rate of relapse increases, after that relatively short period, over the first year to more than 80 percent. What this all means is that currently, only one out of five people will attain sobriety and maintain it for one year. Maintaining sobriety past the first year has an even sharper decline. The high relapse rate for recovering youth is, among other factors, due to the lack of adequate and appropriate aftercare to treatment. If one is fortunate enough to get treatment, there is an unrealistic expectation that after thirty to ninety days of treatment, the individual will be well equipped with skills to maintain sobriety on their own.

Individuals who suffer from psychological disorders are far more likely to relapse than those who do not have any mental health concerns. Mental illness symptoms are not typically of concern in drug treatment, and the same problems that contributed to addiction therefore remain unaddressed and interfere with maintaining sobriety. One study identified several factors such as emotional states and interpersonal and social situations as contributing to relapse (Ramo and Brown 2008). Many people who are fortunate to get some form of treatment are still more likely to relapse and to develop a sense of hopelessness and a negative self-image as a drug addict.

Over the last century, the laws of science and physics have been evolving. Quantum physics describes reality as a component or product of our own perception, and reality is, therefore, full of uncertainties. The concept of model-dependent realism was postulated by physicists (Hawking and Mlodinow 2010). It addresses reality as mental concepts that we create by our interpretation of what we process through our sensory organs and our mind. Reality is essentially a product of our making. From this perspective, the power of positive thinking has a basis on reality and science. These powerful concepts can be applied into a decision to redefine oneself from a negative self-concept created by past behavior into a more positive and future-focused self-image. Hopelessness can turn into hope.

The Stigma of Mental Illness

Historically, in the field of psychotherapy, there has been much focus on pathology, but there have also been schools of thought aimed in a more positive direction. Viktor Emil Frankl was a neurologist and psychiatrist who survived the Holocaust. He valued the positive aspects to being and studied the psychology of striving to create and find meaning in life, no matter how horrible the circumstances. Many of his concepts were derived from studying survivors of the human-created hell on earth also known as the Holocaust. Frankl explored the positive psychological factors of survivors of the Holocaust, who were somehow able to endure unbelievable forms of degradation, torture, and trauma without losing their humanity and faith. He found that many survivors from the camps had in common a belief that there was a purpose for what happened to them. We can learn to use negative experiences in a way to foster self-improvement or establish a new direction in our life. Whether there is a meaning behind negative events or we simply choose to find and create meaning, the result is the same: these events do not need to destroy us; they can make us stronger.

Positive psychology is a branch of cognitive psychology that was developed in the late 1990s by psychologists Martin Seligman and Mihaly Csikszentmihalyi. Similar to humanistic psychology, another positive-focused school of thought, their focus was on understanding the dynamics of mental well-being and psychological growth. Martin Seligman wrote in his book *Authentic Happiness* (2003) about optimism versus pessimism, the importance of identifying one's personal "signature strengths" and developing them to find meaning in one's life rather than focusing on what is wrong or pathological about oneself.

Our society has stigmatized mental illness as well as addiction. The very word "mental illness" has a broad array of negative associations for the average person. Mental illness is a broad and rather vague term. Some feel it is more appropriate and kinder to refer to people who have psychological disorders as "mentally ill," to get away from crude expressions such as "crazy." It is no wonder that adolescents with emotional problems often live in denial of what ails them. No one, especially while in the developmental stage of establishing a self-identity, wants to be thought of or to think of themselves as being "crazy."

When someone uses the crude descriptor "crazy" to refer to someone with mental illness, there is a strong consensus on what that person is describing. "Crazy" brings to mind the ranting, psychopathic stirrings of a lunatic. What does mental illness mean? Due to its being so vague, many people, unfortunately, hold it as having the same meaning as "crazy." The broad term "mental illness" encompasses every psychological problem from anxiety or depression to someone whose thoughts are confused and disorganized and who is not able to differentiate between what is real and not real. Why is there such a narrow-sounding term used to describe a wide spectrum of functioning? The history behind the term "mental illness" will help to clarify and to validate that it is, in fact, an outdated term.

The original application of the term "mental illness" was based on the medical model of pathology. The concept of "mental illness" was derived from the archaic medical concept that psychological problems are merely indicators of a diseased brain (Szasz 1960). Thomas S. Szasz (1960) perhaps best depicts the problematic mentality and negative implications of the medical field's use of the term *mental illness*:

> The notion of mental illness derives its main support from such phenomena as syphilis of the brain or delirious conditions-intoxications, for instance—in which persons are known to manifest various peculiarities or disorders of thinking and behavior. Correctly speaking, however, these are diseases of the brain, not of the mind. According to one school of thought, all so-called mental illness is of this type. (p. 113)
>
> Mental illness has outlived whatever usefulness it might have had and . . . now functions merely as a convenient

myth . . . . The notion of mental illness thus serves mainly to obscure the everyday fact that life for most people is a continuous struggle, not for biological survival, but for a "place in the sun," "peace of mind," or some other human value . . . . Our adversaries are not demons, witches, fate, or mental illness. We have no enemy whom we can fight, exorcise, or dispel by "cure." What we do have are problems in living—whether these be biologic, economic, political, or sociopsychological. (p. 118)

A New Beginning

On the basis of this blurring between what are referred to clinically as "neurotic" versus "psychotic" disorders, I would prefer to not use the term "mental illness" when describing someone who has an affective disorder such as depression or bipolar disorder. Perhaps what is needed is to explain what the modern-day term "mental illness" generally refers to so as to avoid negative connotations. "Mental illness" is, however, currently the correct term to use to refer to someone with psychiatric problems that are impacting and interfering with their everyday existence. For the purpose of this book, the terms "mental illness," "psychological disorder," and "mental disorder" are therefore used to refer to people who have mild, moderate, and even severe psychiatric symptoms.

Mild to moderate mental health disorders of focus include depression, anxiety, mood, and bipolar disorders that can be stabilized by medication management. Individuals suffering from such psychiatric symptoms are likely to benefit from an intensive outpatient treatment center to address their co-occurring disorders. Individuals with more severe and unstable mental disorders are more likely to benefit from a more intensive inpatient treatment center until their symptoms can be stabilized. If there is no such facility available, then supportive therapy and medication management can be implemented. Closer monitoring of symptoms and adherence to their medication management as well as coordination with any and all family and community support available is necessary for treatment of more severe disorders.

No one should be turned away from treatment if they are believed to be at high risk of harming themselves or others. The individual cannot simply be turned away or left on their own. Individuals who struggle with more severe psychiatric symptoms and a substance disorder are in a much higher risk category for suicide potential and must be carefully and repeatedly assessed for suicidal thoughts. Can you imagine how hopeless it would feel to be turned away from an attempt to reach out for help? "No wrong door" means just that: access to an appropriate level of care, wherever that might be, is an essential component to our mission (SAMHSA 2011, 11). Individuals who are actively using may make overtly manipulative threats of self-harm, but all statements involving a threat of self-harm must be taken seriously (SAMHSA 2011, ch. 4, pgs. 76-77). Active use and especially relapse can result in feelings of despair and desperation as well as more impulsive and risky behaviors.

The screening and evaluation stage of treatment should take into account any underlying thought disorders, both acute and chronic, as well as minimization of symptoms. Adolescents tend to minimize their symptoms and to hide suicidal thoughts. This requires the clinician to be thorough and competent in their initial evaluation. Many teens with a longer history of using substances often have secret thoughts and feelings of immortality and magical thinking. People with magical thinking believe that things can be undone. Sometimes they believe that they are immortal and that suicide will not end their life and are therefore at a greater risk of self-harm.

Addiction and mental illness are unfortunately highly correlated to suicide. Suicidal thoughts and statements cannot be washed over and ignored. Suicidal thoughts or statements indicating feelings of hopelessness should be considered as high-risk indicators for potential suicidal behavior, especially for an adolescent with depression and anxiety who is also struggling with addiction. The concept "suicidal gesture" is a misnomer; gestures are really incomplete attempts at best. Suicidal thoughts are not always expressed as desire to die as much as feelings of hopelessness. Craving or withdrawal from the effects of any drug is always a high-risk situation, and many completed suicides occur during the withdrawal phase.

Lastly, despite any conflicted feelings you may have, it is far better to get help if someone you know appears depressed or hopeless and jokes about suicide and risk their anger than to wait for the worst to happen. Such calls are taken seriously and can be made anonymously. People do not talk or joke about killing themselves unless they are in a lot of emotional pain. There is great ambivalence in suicidal thoughts, which is why any self-harming behavior is never a "gesture" but a strong signal of what is to come.

Other behaviors may be indicators that someone is thinking of ending their life. Increased isolation, lack of interest in doing things that used to be fun for them, lack of appetite, not taking care of themselves, unusual bruising or unexplained marks or cuts on their bodies, giving things away, and even reminiscing about better days could be subtle hints that an individual is moving in a direction that may end with them taking their own life. Suicidal thoughts occur when someone feels there is no hope, no way out, and may even believe that others will be better off without them. There is no logic involved with suicidal thoughts, however; it is pure emotion.

Despite thoughts that suicide is the only solution to stop their pain, suicidal adolescents need to understand that suicide is never a solution. It is a dark hole opening up in the ground that swallows all loving survivors whole. Where there is life, there is hope. Sadly, when someone is feeling suicidal, they cannot see this fact. Death is the great equalizer; it is a permanent decision for a temporary problem. If you have any concern about your friend or family member being at risk for suicide, take whatever steps are necessary to keep them safe. It is better to risk their anger than to lose their companionship forever.

None of the above is written to discourage, only to increase awareness of the very real setbacks to sobriety. Although it is always possible to achieve recovery from addiction, it takes more time, effort, and support the longer the addiction continues. Addiction and mental health symptoms left untreated become more unyielding over time. Recovery is a process in which this process is slowly reversed. Just as it took time to develop the addiction, it takes time to undo the effects. The sooner treatment can begin, the better the outcome.

The first step in the process of recovery is awareness. Awareness of the problem and that there is a solution, that help and support are available, and that you can regain control of your life. Awareness that you are important and that your life and your future, no matter how fractured and hopeless you think things might have become, have tremendous value. Value to you, to your friends and family, and to others whose life you have yet to touch.

We all grow and develop differently; no two people are alike. No one has the magical ability or power to read your mind. Only you know your true thoughts, feelings, and fears. No one else can tell you how you feel or should feel. You are the true expert of yourself. You can fool everyone, even yourself if you wish, but to be totally honest with yourself and others is instrumental to self-improvement and success in your recovery. Recovery can be a painful experience at times, but that is when you need to allow others to provide support and help you through your darkest moments. No one needs to go through the process alone.

This book is intended for everyone to increase their understanding of addiction, just as it is for anyone who suffers from addiction to know that recovery is possible. For a successful outcome to treatment, you need to dismiss negative self-perceptions and doubts you may have about yourself. Forget any criticisms or hurtful things people may have said or done to you in the past. Remember that it is easier for people to condemn or dismiss others than it is for them to look within, so let it all go and focus on your own very unique journey.

PART TWO

Understanding

Adolescent Development

Adolescence is perhaps the most psychologically and physically challenging developmental period of modern human life. It is no small wonder that the peak years of suicide attempts occur during adolescence. When does childhood end and adolescence begin? More precisely, what defines the conclusion of each developmental phase of childhood, adolescence, and the successful transition to adulthood? In earlier stages of humanity's development, the stages of childhood and adulthood were more clearly defined and understood at a collective level.

In past societies, adolescence was viewed as a relatively brief and meaningless period of time between childhood and adulthood. Children often worked and were expected to survive as adults well before age eighteen. There was no formal education for the lower socioeconomic "masses" and certainly not any expectation of schooling past learning how to read and write, if that. Marriage and becoming parents occurred at a much younger age than the current norm in modernized cultures. The overall expectations were that once the stage that we now identify as adolescence arrived, all the freedoms and restrictions of childhood were essentially over.

Life was certainly harder from a survival perspective, but simpler in execution as there were far fewer options. Social expectations for the working class were for one to make a living as a farmer or apprentice to a trade, to marry (although legalized "civil" marriage is in itself a relatively modern concept), and to raise children. People lived their entire lives in small and relatively isolated communities.

There was no mass transit, automobiles, television, telephones, radio, or Internet. Exposure to new people, ideas, and ways of living were limited. Adolescents didn't have to struggle with choosing from a wide array of life choices. You were usually born into your occupation, and often, marriages were arranged by your parents for property or other considerations during childhood. Although this might seem brutal, contrary to popular opinion, more choices do not always result in greater happiness, and in fact, it is usually the opposite.

As humankind advanced and society developed from an agrarian-based lifestyle to the present industrial and technologically based lifestyle, there has been an increased demand for education and technical training. Higher education was no longer restricted to a select aristocratic few. This increased demand for education and for technological training extended the period of adolescence and delayed the demands as well as freedoms of adulthood. The concept of adolescence, therefore, is still in a relatively early anthropological stage of humankind's development. Our advancements and technology have surpassed the speed of evolutionary and neurological development of the adolescent mind.

To add to the frustration, there is also a difference in the average rate of neurological development between males and females; the average male takes more time than the average female to fully develop neurologically. Males are typically two years behind females in neurological development and do not typically catch up until their twenties. This doesn't in any way imply that females are superior; what it does suggest is that the demands of life and academia during childhood and adolescence are often greater for the average male than for the average female.

This knowledge about gender differences in neurological development unfortunately has not made its way into most elementary school academia, and teacher expectations generally do not take real developmental differences between the sexes into account. For some, this perceived "delay" has been misconstrued as the child (typically male) having an attention deficit or a learning disability. Consequently, there is a disproportionate amount of boys with normal intelligence placed into special education programs. This practice results in frustration, low self-esteem, and possible mislabeling as "learning disabled" for many who may not be. Contrary to commonsense expectation, many special education teachers really are not sufficiently trained to provide the individualized education necessary for children who have specific learning disabilities, and if there is a disability, it is not typically accurately addressed.

In addition to this, many children with "attention deficits" due to anxiety and those who have learning disorders are too often placed into the same "special education" classroom as children who were separated from the mainstream population for aggressive bullying behavior. It is no wonder that when these anxious or truly learning-disabled young people reach adolescence, they are saddled with confusion, frustration, anger, and often a feeling of hopelessness. All these contribute to the perfect brew for low self-esteem and feelings of isolation and loneliness, with a burning desire to be accepted by their peers. The result of this quest for peer approval and acceptance is, too often, associating with older marginalized individuals, unsafe sexual practices with multiple partners, poor grades or dropping out of school, criminal behavior, and drug use.

Adolescence has been understood by many generations as a difficult period of life to move through. This already sensitive period becomes more difficult when the adolescent must deal with a developing mental illness, which adds an extra layer to the challenge of adolescence. When an adolescent with depression, anxiety, or mood swings succumbs to drug use, development of higher cognitive functions including impulse control and decision-making skills are hampered, negative shifts in peer associations occur, and mental health symptoms worsen. Depression, anxiety, unstable moods, and thought disorders are enough of a challenge to overcome; combining this with drug use increases the level of chaos exponentially. The sooner the individual can pull out of this potential downward spiral, the better their chance of a full recovery and normal neurological and physical development.

Brain Development

Our brain is part of our central nervous system and is the master controller of our body. The human brain is similar to the brains of other animals, but with a greater degree of complexity and neural connections. The human brain is organized into five main sections, and within each section are subdivisions that in turn contain communicating tracts or nerves and groups of neurons called nuclei or ganglia. The various ganglia are responsible for different functions, including pleasure. We will briefly examine the brain structures or nuclei that are involved in the sensation of pleasure and in the development of addiction.

Over the millennium, the human brain is the product of more complex brain structures developing from the original primitive reptilian brain. However, there are still components or brain structures similar to our more primitive origins. For the sake of simplicity, imagine that there are three layers of the human brain. The first "layer" is the primitive brain, which contains the brain stem that controls our automatic functions (such as breathing). No conscious thought is required for this brain system to operate. The next "layer" is our limbic system, which is made up of groups of nerve cells (nuclei) that interact with each other and, among other functions, are involved with learning, memory, and emotion. The last "layer" to have developed is the cerebral cortex, responsible for higher levels of brain function such as decision making, judgment, and analytic and abstractive thinking. The further up the evolutionary chain of mammals, the larger and more complex this part of the brain is.

The primary difference between a human brain and other mammals is the size and complexity of the cerebral cortex. More primitive animals such as reptiles do not have a cerebral cortex. Their brain is comprised primarily of the primitive brain, which means they do not have to think or process information to react. The concept of "fight or flight" (Cannon 1929) is a primitive brain response to acute distress. This automatic response to a perceived threat arises from the reptilian or primitive brain center in our brain for which immediate survival is the only concern. The reptilian brain is relatively simple and has successfully developed for survival only. Unlike people, a reptile does not have emotions or cognitive thought and reacts to the environment without thought.

To be a bit more technical, the brain can be broken down into subdivisions that parallel both evolutionary development of our species and embryonic neural development. These are the brain stem, the cerebellum, the cerebrum, and its subdivisions including the cerebral cortex, the thalamus, and the hypothalamus. In amphibians, fish, and reptiles, the cerebrum plays the predominant role involved with survival. In reptiles, there is a small neural tissue or neocortex, which is a relatively insignificant part of the reptilian brain. In mammals and particularly in humans, the neocortex is folded or convoluted and therefore much larger, playing a more predominant role in behavior. Complexity of behavior is directly correlated with the larger cortex as is the ability to have cognition or thought. Humans, unlike reptiles, have higher brain functions such as metacognition, the ability to be aware of one's own thoughts.

The limbic system and basal ganglia are part of the cerebral hemispheres. The basal ganglia, among other roles, are involved in motor control. The amygdala is a nuclei body that is part of this system of ganglia. The limbic system is involved with emotions, learning, and memory. The hippocampus is another very important group of brain nuclei in this limbic system.

This may sound complicated, but what is most relevant for our purposes is that the amygdala and the hippocampus play essential roles in our emotional behavior. Simply put, the amygdala is what drives fear and anger and is regulated by the hippocampus and our neocortex. In a reptile, a behavioral reaction to a perceived threat is to kill or escape. For humans, with our more complex brains, the choice of behavioral responses is also more complex. This is both a blessing and a curse and underlines much of our psychological woes.

To sum up the primary difference in maturation between the human brain and the reptilian brain, a reptile, due to its simple neurology, is born already "knowing" how to survive. Humans take a lot longer to develop into psychologically mature and capable adults. Adolescence is an important part of this developmental process. It is the developmental period when higher forms of thinking and reasoning start to take root.

We will examine how psychological disorders or mental illness are involved with drug abuse, but right now let us discuss why it is relevant and important to understand what happens when a substance is introduced into your blood and, ultimately, your brain. Most illicit drugs and alcohol interfere with the executive functioning of the frontal lobes. This includes judgment, impulse control, and the filter effect of reasoning on our more primitive brain functions. As previously discussed, the primary distinguishing feature of the human brain from the reptilian brain is our enormous cerebral hemisphere and our limbic system safeguards such as the hippocampus. Essentially, when you become intoxicated, what makes you human is anesthetized. You are operating with only your emotional and impulsive reptilian brain.

When under the influence of mind-altering substances, people will typically lose their normal self-restraint and impulse control. They are acting under the control of their reptilian brain mixed with the lesser aspects of their emotional brain. Many individuals under the influence of an intoxicating substance engage in behaviors that are atypical for them, such as deception, theft, or destructive behavior, which can have serious and sometimes fatal consequences not only for themselves but also for others.

Some individuals have described their behavior while deep in their addiction as having "lost their souls," meaning that they no longer operate under their normal "moral code." A reality check in regard to using any intoxicating and mind-altering substance is to know that whenever you choose to ingest, smoke, snort, or inject something to "numb you out," you give up your conscious choice of behavior and control over any potential consequences and outcome of being under the influence. As a result of your impulsive and intoxicated behavior, you put in harm's way not only yourself, but potentially other victims as well. The consequences can, in some cases, be life altering especially if your behavior results in someone else losing their life. Very recently, a young man tragically lost his life in my neighborhood due to someone else being intoxicated behind the wheel of a car. Life for the victim, the driver, and their families were forever altered in a way that can never be repaired.

Genetics and environmental stimulation are correlated with intelligence. It is well accepted that neurological development is crucial during infancy and early childhood and that the environment plays a large role in this development. We now understand that full neurological development can extend into the early twenties and perhaps into the mid to late twenties for males. Drug use during neural development can hamper the full development of fundamentally important brain functions such as impulse control and decision making.

Jay Giedd is a neuroscientist at the National Institute of Mental Health. He proposed that adolescence is just as critical in the overall development of brain neurology as is early childhood. Brain development during adolescence, according to Dr. Giedd, is greatly impacted by activities the individual engages in during adolescence (Giedd 2011). He proposed that a limitation of environmental stimuli during adolescence can reduce optimal neurological development.

Drug use during adolescence interferes in different ways with normal development. Neurological development occurs from the back of the brain (primarily responsible for motor control) to the front (responsible for executive brain functions such as judgment, impulse control, and decision making). During adolescence, the frontal lobes are still developing. The frontal lobes are largely responsible for what is termed executive functioning: decision making, impulse control, judgment, and paying attention. Drug use can interfere with normal neurological development. However, due to the neuroplasticity (ability of the brain to compensate and redirect neural connections) and neurogenesis (replacement of dead neurons with the growth of new neurons from stem cells in our brains) of our brain, this is not cause for despair but, clearly, added justification to stop using.

We are still learning about neurogenesis, how the human brain is able to regenerate, repair, and redirect to compensate for neural damage throughout the life span. In addition to plasticity or the ability to form new dendritic connections to compensate for lost connections, our brain has stem cells that can actually generate new neurons. Despite this potential for regrowth, the more extensive and chronic the damage, the less able the brain will be to fully heal itself. It is far better to free oneself of addiction earlier than later for many reasons, this being just one more reason.

Here is the bad news: not all drugs are alike, and some are more damaging than others. Some drugs such as methamphetamine can cause instantaneous and extensive neurological damage, perhaps more so than all other drugs. Likewise, excessive alcoholic binging actually kills off stem cells within the brain that are responsible for neurogenesis. Although all drugs affect and potentially damage different organs in our body in distinct ways, some seem to wreak more havoc on the brain than others. Despite being legal, chronic and excessive use of alcohol causes the most pervasive organ damage of any intoxicating substance. However, although alcohol can be more damaging over a longer period of time, methamphetamine and other synthetic drugs such as ecstasy can do more extensive neurological damage in a far shorter period of time.

Ecstasy is currently considered to be one of the most popular club drugs and, due to its inducement of euphoria and hypersexuality, has become a risk factor in the spread of HIV. Ecstasy has made the news due to its potential to cause rapid physiological changes that can result in instantaneous death. A little known fact, however, is that use of club drugs such as ecstasy has another potentially lethal risk factor as their use greatly increases the risk of spreading sexually transmitted diseases such as HIV. Under the influence of ecstasy, sex appears to be more spontaneous, occurring without planning or use of protection. The practice of unprotected sex while under the influence is so high that HIV has now made a dramatic comeback, with the new highest risk group for contracting HIV occurring in the *heterosexual adolescent* population.

Heroin, methamphetamine, and cocaine are no winners either, as they can do considerable damage to the cardiovascular system. Heroin and methamphetamine are also frequently administered through injection, which also increases the risk of spreading HIV. Cocaine is so instantaneously damaging to the heart that autopsies can reveal the amount and frequency of cocaine use by examination of the extent of subsequent damage to the heart. Heroin also causes considerable damage over time to the liver, the heart, and bone density. As mentioned previously, methamphetamine causes extensive neurological damage as well as damage to the lungs. Cannabis, considered by many to be a "natural" and therefore harmless drug, is actually more damaging to the lungs than cigarettes, and a fact unknown to most is that it increases the risk of cancer. Cannabis can also result in a psychological condition known as "amotivational syndrome," which results in the individual, over time, losing their natural incentive to achieve.

The sooner one stops abusing substances, the faster and more complete the recovery to more healthy brain functioning. Additionally, as we are all different and have different limitations, the frequency and level of drug use that may not "fry" your friend's brain or result in their death may very well do you in. You won't know what the level of resilience your body and your brain has until after the fact, and at that point, you probably will no longer be aware of the full extent of the damage. It is, however, never too early or too late to stop.

Perhaps more relevant, given the natural resilience of the adolescents' brains, is that even if there is no noticeable long-term organic damage, a pattern of drug use as a primary coping mechanism for avoidance of emotional pain interferes with normal psychological and social development. Adolescents who learn to rely on substances to deal with stress are not learning how to cope with life's stress without numbing themselves. This is another real problem that occurs from extensive drug use that starts during adolescence. Individuals can become stuck in a cycle of using substances and falling back into addiction as the primary and perhaps only method of coping with life's curveballs. Sobriety without developing adequate coping skills sets the stage for the recovering individual's next relapse. Successful recovery therefore requires learning new cognitive and social skills to deal with life.

PART THREE

The Snake Who Swallowed Its Tail

Cycle of Addiction

As I have interacted with individuals suffering from substance abuse disorders for many years, it has become clear to me that "kicking" the actual physical addiction, although a miserable experience in itself, is a relatively small part to the overall difficulty someone who struggles with addiction must face. The larger challenge is remaining sober and relearning how to live in this world without the toxic but familiar crutch of addiction. Most people with substance abuse disorders have been using their drug of choice as an attempt to self-comfort or "numb" out for an extended period of time. For many, ambivalence about getting clean is due to a fear of how they will manage without their drug of choice.

The act of using becomes a familiar way of life, like a comfortable old blanket. Despite their awareness of the destructive forces of their addiction and a desire to stop using, it has become the only coping strategy many have come to rely on and know. It is actually the fear of the unknown, living clean and sober, and a belief that they cannot succeed that throws many back into relapse.

Most people suffering from addiction have never successfully learned other healthier means of self-soothing. They typically began their journey into addiction at a surprisingly young and developmentally immature age. Statistics indicate that drug use begins around age fourteen, but more often, anecdotal statements indicate introduction to substance abuse, including alcohol, is closer to the age of eleven. Additionally, most non-drug-using methods of coping with life's woes someone addicted may have had are forgotten.

Once an individual finds him or herself immersed in their addiction, they forget who they are and begin to narrowly define themselves as nothing more than an addict or, more harshly, as a "stone-cold junkie." Daily life becomes focused on obtaining whatever will numb them out. The focus is on getting money to buy their drug of choice. Obtaining, using, and withdrawing becomes a daily ritual, and once this sequence is completed, they start the cycle all over again, spiraling into an ever-deeper level of demoralization and sense of hopelessness.

Historically, many different treatments have surfaced, some more successful than others. Differences in the most recognized treatment approaches for addiction have been based on dramatically different theoretical concepts. The primary distinction between the more recognized theories is the predilection of viewing addiction from a genetic, behavioral, or disease model. While the different theories may recognize other factors involved in addiction, these factors are generally neither addressed nor integrated into a more holistic and dynamic approach to understanding and treating addiction.

Several ideologies have developed over time, some with more success than others. An older and outdated philosophy had the core belief that if the "addict" really wanted to conquer their addiction, they would succeed; a lack of willpower and character were held as the primary reason for relapse. This school of thought put the entire weight of sobriety on the shoulders of the individual and promoted the concept that only people of weak character succumbed to addiction.

Other more supportive 12-step programs developed a disease-based model with the belief that an individual could not conquer their addiction unless they surrendered themselves to a higher power and engaged with a supportive network of others who struggle with the same demon, so to speak. This program's success rate seems to vary between studies but has been demonstrated to have a better success rate than most other available single-focus treatments. However, this program requires a strong religious or spiritual conviction. People with a more secular philosophy could not follow the concept of a higher power and developed other models. Unfortunately, many of the alternative programs again placed success primarily on willpower, intelligence, and character, none of which have been supported by research.

Medical models came into the front line with a biologically based perspective of addiction. Advances in neurology and genetics allowed researchers to better understand addiction. The emphasis was placed on genetics, with psychopharmaceuticals as the method of treatment. Addiction was seen as a genetically programmed phenomenon, and that some people are born with a propensity to develop addiction and therefore are at a higher risk for developing addiction. When integrated with other treatment methods, pharmaceutical interventions can be invaluable.

Our society has become enamored, however, with pharmaceuticals and medicine, and there has been a push in the medical field to treat every ailment that humankind encounters with medication. Medical science and neurology became the top runners in the race toward finding "the cure" for addiction. The problem with this focus is that it does not take into account all the factors that contribute to drug use and addiction. Fortunately, medical research is now beginning to recognize and incorporate conjunctive treatments, including therapy, and more holistic methods to treat disease, including motivating changes in behavior.

Research identified neurological components involved with addiction, and the search for the magic bullet involving pharmaceutical intervention began. Medication was developed to help people achieve physical detoxification and abstinence with varying degrees of success. Neurologists became the new gurus and overly simplified addiction into abnormalities of brain structures and deficiencies of neurotransmitters. Some medications came into being that should theoretically prevent relapse. Yet treatment with medications alone, which interfere with the sensation of euphoria from a dopamine substance and diminish the physical craving for that substance by acting on the dopamine receptors in the brain, still only result in less than a 50 percent rate of continued abstinence for less than ninety days.

The rate of relapse increases over time just as it does for other single-approach treatments of addiction. Although medication has been demonstrated to be an important component in the treatment of mental illness and addiction, the incorporation of multiple methods is clearly indicated. Treatment of addiction, especially as a co-occurring disorder, is a much more complicated problem than any singularly focused approach can solve.

Although neurology is clearly an essential component in understanding and treating addiction, the science of neurology is still in its infancy. Anyone familiar with doing research and running statistics knows that in any research study, statistics can be manipulated, and there will always be confounding variables making it difficult to pinpoint exact causation. These variables can make something look different from what it really is by providing false statistical results and therefore an inaccurate cause and effect. Unfortunately, there have been claims made by researchers in various fields of science that are later revealed to have been inaccurate, to say the least, based on a flawed research design or a purposeful misapplication of statistics. Although we are gaining a better understanding of the human brain and many of the neurological and chemical factors involved in addiction, holding neurology as providing the definitive answer is too restrictive. Addiction has a multifaceted etiology, and neurological factors are only part of the problem of addiction.

Environmental factors affecting the individual, such as financial, social, and cultural factors, can contribute to the probability of developing an addiction as well as add to the difficulties of achieving and maintaining sobriety. The age at which one begins using the substance and any consequences or nonconsequences as a result of their usage will also determine the likelihood of later addiction. Additionally, how accessible and accepted a particular substance is to an individual's circle of family and friends is a very real factor in predicting outcome.

A propensity for developing an addiction may also be due to genetic factors, although it is difficult to factor out the confounding variable of social learning. Alcoholism is addiction to alcohol and has been studied perhaps more than other types of addiction. Does someone become an alcoholic because their parents drank and they have the same underlying genetics and neurology, or is it because they were abused and neglected by their addicted, alcoholic parents and developed depression and poor coping skills? Role modeling after their parents that drinking is an acceptable coping mechanism can also factor in as a contributing cause for developing alcoholism.

The answer to the primary cause for developing alcoholism, just as for other addictions, is not clear; what is clear is that there is some correlation between addiction and family of origin. Children of alcoholics appear to be at greater risk of developing addictions themselves. There has been some indication that people who experiment with drugs and had been abused as children are more likely to develop a substance abuse disorder than their associates who had not suffered similar childhood abuse. It is not yet clear, however, if this is because they were abused by their parents or because their addicted parents were abusive while under the influence (Mitchell and Lawrence 2011), having been addicts themselves, and therefore the primary cause is genetic, more so than environmental.

Although there has been considerable research and investment into gaining insight as to how to improve the effectiveness of the treatment of addiction, the current rate of sustained recovery is unacceptable, and the cost to our youth, their families, and society is immeasurable. Although many branches of government, education, social services, law, and mental health providers are involved at some level in helping adolescents with mental health and substance abuse disorders, progress continues to falter. There is a need for a greater coordination and collaborative effort between all involved agencies, yet despite the awareness by some of this need, there is a void in the actual community. As stated in a recent publication by the US Department of Health and Human Services, Substance Abuse and Mental Health Services Administration Center for Substance Abuse Treatment, "many providers and agencies are responsible for the care, protection, or support of young people: the child welfare, education, and juvenile justice systems, as well as medical and mental health care providers and community organizations. Yet resources within these agencies are scattered, not coordinated, and often do not effectively support prevention programs or policies. The result is a patchwork that does not perform as an integrated system and fails to serve the needs of many young people and their families" (SAMHSA 2011).

The treatment protocol presented in this book is founded on a core set of practice principles that are termed "evidence-based practice" (SAMHSA 2009, module 1:1, 16). Evidenced-based treatment is an integrated system derived from research as a more comprehensive and effective way to treat individuals with co-occurring disorders. The system addresses the complex problem of treatment of individuals with co-occurring disorders. This is important because a substantial portion of people suffering from addiction also suffers from mental illness (SAMHSA 2011).

Evidence-based treatment has been specifically designed to address the needs of individuals with co-occurring mental health and substance abuse disorders. An important element to this system is assessing the level of severity for both disorders and tailoring the treatment program to meet these dual challenges to treatment. Ongoing evaluation of the individual through the course of treatment ensures that treatment remains fluid and adjusts to the particular needs of whatever stage of denial, readiness, or recovery the individual may be in.

An additional difficulty in the treatment of addiction lies in problems of addiction-related cognition and learned behaviors. Someone who has been using a substance over a period of time may never fully develop or can lose a previous level of capacity to regulate their emotional reactions and emotional states, also commonly referred to as coping skills. Deficits in coping skills often result in a negatively reinforcing loop of an addiction cycle. This loop is evoked when dealing with a perceived negative event (actual or imagined) and by remembering past experiences of substance abuse that temporarily diminished previous emotionally painful states. The individual then craves the substance that they believe to have previously numbed their negative emotional state, providing them with real or imagined temporary relief.

Addiction, therefore, is negatively reinforced; it removes a painful experience and therefore is a powerful force to contend with. The individual believes that use of the substance will, at least temporarily, reduce their emotional pain. This is perhaps the biggest obstacle to establishing sustained recovery or abstinence. Among other obstacles to recovery, one must learn how to sit out a negative state until it passes, to distract from the awful emotional feeling, to reduce the severity of that emotion, and learn to cope with future negative events and emotions without using. After addiction sets in, it is more than a matter of willpower; it is getting the treatment, skills, and confidence that you can get through it without using that are all necessary to address the multifarious and unending problems life presents.

What works for one person may not work as well for another who may require a different combination of treatment strategies. There is, however, no absolute failure, only setbacks, on the road to sustained recovery. People may feel discouraged when they enter a treatment program and relapse. It is more likely, however, that rather than a personal "failure," the program wasn't suited for them or they might not have been ready for full, sustained recovery. A careful evaluation by a competent and caring (key words) clinician and honest introspection, however, will move someone with an addiction on to the right path. Perceived "failure," shame, and discouragement only fuel the cycle of addiction, and therefore, careless or inappropriate treatment can reduce an individual's chance for achieving sustained recovery.

Other important factors involved in the development and maintenance of an addiction is one's psychological state at the time of their first use of a substance. If the psychological problems that predated the addiction are not addressed, recovery can be sabotaged. Contrary to the misperception entertained by many who have been fortunate to have never developed a substance abuse disorder, a large percentage of young people typically experimented with substances because they were trying to escape from a negative emotional state that had engulfed them for a period of time. In addition to this, use of substances to achieve emotional numbing typically occurs without any introspective awareness. It is a lot easier to convince yourself that you use because it is fun than to admit you are attempting to escape from emotional pain, feelings of despair, anxiety, or something seemingly simple such as social phobia.

We live in an increasingly detached and socially disconnected world. The ease of entering worlds of fantastic escape via television, the Internet, and electronic gaming, just to name a few, has made it socially acceptable at some level to avoid real and genuine social interaction. Drug and alcohol addiction are growing exponentially not only due to the increased availability of these substances but also perhaps as a result of a sense of isolation, despair, and hopelessness. Our increasingly detached and complicated world is more difficult for some than others to manage through, especially if they are suffering from anxiety, depression, or cognitive challenges. Add to that the general instability of mood experienced by many adolescents due to hormonal changes, personal struggles with self-esteem, and challenges of transitioning to adulthood, and it should be understandable that drug abuse and addiction often follow "experimentation."

Keep an open mind while you read this. Try to put aside negativity, criticism, and any type of condemnation about people who suffer from addiction, especially if it is you. The purpose of this book is to educate and to enlighten as well as to give hope and useful direction to people with addictions and to those who care for them and want to help but feel lost and helpless.

Have hope as it is never too late. If you are suffering from addiction, try to imagine that you are a once again a young child, a perfect, innocent human being who is only looking ahead. No looking back, only looking forward. It is also important to forgive others if you can for whatever slights they may have done to you, imagined or real, as anger is a powerful self-destructive emotion. More importantly, forgive yourself for any of your perceived or real imperfections as a human being. It is time for you to climb up and out of the rabbit hole of addiction.

Defining Addiction
(Substance Abuse Disorders)

Many studies have been done to answer questions regarding the cause of addiction. It is now known that genetics and environment are both involved in addiction, but it is still unclear, however, which is the stronger factor. It is evident that there is a genetic predisposition of underlying neurological structures that predispose some individuals for addiction. Additionally, the earlier an individual begins using addictive substances the more vulnerable they are to develop addiction as their brain is relatively immature and vulnerable to modification from prolonged drug use. Modifications in the reward system of the brain due to substance abuse increase dependency on that substance and maintain the addictive cycle. It is clear, however, that even when an individual may have a genetic predisposition for addiction, they can overcome this if they are motivated, through effective treatment of their co-occurring disorder.

Mental and addictive disorders are medical disorders and, in reality, are no different from many other medical disorders. Using the analogy of other medical disorders, such as diabetes or high blood pressure, not everyone with the predisposition to developing these disorders will succumb to the full impact of these disorders. Lifestyle changes with or without medication can often successfully hedge off the long-term devastation and havoc caused by these disorders. The same is true for mental and addictive disorders. Inversely, addiction can increase psychiatric symptoms and, in some cases, contribute to the development of mental disorders.

According to the *Diagnostic and Statistical Manual of Mental Disorders, Fourth Edition, Text Revision* (*DSM-IV-TR*), the standard clinical diagnostic manual used by mental health practitioners (American Psychiatric Association 2000), addiction is identified as substance dependence. In the *DSM-IV-TR*, substance dependence is defined as "a cluster of cognitive, behavioral and physiological symptoms indicating the continuous use of the substance despite significant substance-related problems" (p. 192). Essentially, once physical and psychological dependency on a particular substance occurs, an individual can have great difficulty stopping even when it is apparent that continuing to use is contraindicated by the negative consequences already experienced from using.

Dependence on a substance is identified in the *DSM-IV-TR* as when an individual engages in self-defeating use of a substance despite negative consequences. More specifically, dependency is defined as occurring over the course of a minimum of one year, during which the individual exhibits three or more symptoms or a "cluster" of specific symptoms. These symptoms include the development of tolerance or a decreased response to a particular substance and therefore a greater need for that substance to induce a particular desired effect, and withdrawal symptoms after cessation of the substance, including physiological pain and problems with perception and cognition, which result in craving of the substance with a desire to return to what has become the individual's perception of "normalcy."

Other indicators of addiction include increased use (frequency and amount) and repeated, unsuccessful attempts to control or stop use of the substance. The substance begins to dominate the individual's life to an extent that attempts to attain and to use the substance become the individual's focus of existence. Ultimately, other activities, interests, responsibilities, and relationships are abandoned in the pursuit of the substance. Lastly, use of the substance continues despite an awareness of the negative consequences and previous attempts to stop. The drug of choice becomes the individual's new best friend, their primary "relationship," and their sole focus of existence.

A stand-up comedian once made a poignant joke regarding his personal struggle with addiction: "No one could imagine getting angry at someone with a medical disorder like diabetes . . . so why do they get angry at you for having an addiction?" Addiction has been defined as a medical disorder, with the perspective that addiction is a chronic and progressive disease. Some medical practitioners view addiction as a "brain disease" and that treatment should be held at the same level of medical treatment as for other chronic diseases. In this school of thought, addictive disorders are viewed as a medical disorder and are classified as substance abuse disorders. Substance abuse disorders compare similarly to other chronic medical conditions, which include type 1 diabetes, hypertension, and asthma. Genetics and environmental factors such as lifestyle are also implicated with the incidence of these disorders. Compliance with treatment among many patients with chronic medical disorders is below recommended levels, and the rate of relapse or return of symptoms is equally high. Noncompliance and relapse in addictive disorders likewise should be treated, as are other medical disorders, as temporary setbacks rather than failure (McClellan et al. 2000).

The National Institute on Drug Abuse (NIDA) similarly compared addiction treatment with treatment of hypertension (NIDA 2009). This study noted that in the treatment of hypertension, there is a baseline of symptoms, and typically during the course of treatment, there will be a reduction in symptoms. If treatment is discontinued, there is a return of symptoms, but treatment is still viewed as successful because during treatment, symptoms were reduced. Treatment of chronic medical disorders such as hypertension is viewed as symptom management. If during the course of treatment there is a return of symptoms, the treatment is not considered a failure but indicative of a reevaluation of treatment needs.

Conversely, in the treatment of addiction, a relapse or return of symptoms is typically erroneously viewed as failure. Treatment is considered to have been unsuccessful, or the patient is viewed as not fully committed to treatment. Based on available research, however, treatment of addictive disorders requires a paradigm shift (change in perspective) in the medical and mental health community to view treatment of addiction as similar to the treatment of other chronic medical disorders. In this revised framework paralleling other medical disorders, a lapse or relapse and return of symptoms signifies that *treatment* needs be reevaluated. If the approach to treatment of addiction is similar to that of other chronic disorders, the negative connotation of treatment or individual failure would be replaced with a more positive, long-term approach and movement toward symptom management with the goal of reduction of symptoms and substance dependency.

Despite this, substance abuse disorders and noncompliance with recommended treatment are held by many health care providers and the general population as an indication of a lack of willpower or character. A substance abuse disorder is still not understood or viewed as a medical disorder. This is unfortunate—if the health care community treated addiction with the same vigor as treatment of other medical disorders, the success rate of sustained sobriety would likely increase.

Currently, people with substance abuse disorders are often treated with more disdain than concern by the health care community. The stigma for individuals with a substance abuse disorder often throws a roadblock to that individual in receiving the same level of treatment for other medical conditions they may have as are nonaddicts. More often than not, their report of pain or other symptoms are disregarded and typically dismissed as drug-seeking behavior. This phenomenon of dismissal of human suffering has also been from health concerns that have arisen from a lack of provided appropriate medical treatment by health care providers that are provided to "normal" people (McClellan 2000).

Unfortunately, not only is addiction generally dismissed and stigmatized by the medical community, mental health disorders are also often overlooked, not diagnosed, or simply dismissed as adolescent "acting out" and ultimately ignored. The comorbidity rate of mental health disorders and addiction (which means how often they occur together) has been verified by research, yet treatment has not effectively been addressed within the general medical or mental health community.

Addictive disorders, especially for adolescents, are effectively not typically covered by insurance for any inpatient treatment other than medical detoxification. Outpatient treatment for adolescents is typically not covered and therefore not affordable for most low- and middle-income families. Most commonly available adolescent treatments such as short-term day treatment or drug education do not adequately address both mental illness and substance abuse and therefore do not address co-occurring disorders.

The phenomenon of co-occurring disorders has a devastating consequence on the individual and on their family. Dual diagnosis or co-occurring disorders refers to an individual who has a psychological disorder, such as depression or other psychological problem, and a substance abuse disorder at the same time. As mentioned earlier, substance abuse not only increases psychiatric symptoms but can also obscure the presence of a mental disorder, as many health care providers write off psychiatric symptoms as due only to substance abuse.

As examined earlier, there are biological reasons that explain why and how this combination of an addictive and mental disorder can occur. Through a combination of experimentation and peer influence, someone suffering from depression or anxiety discovers that certain substances give them a "quick fix" and seemingly reduce their emotionally painful symptoms. Over time there is an increased reliance of the drug, and use of the substance becomes a more frequent behavior. Tolerance develops, and before awareness of dependency on the drug occurs, addiction takes hold.

No one ever thinks that they will become addicted; it is never planned or intentional. Addiction is often a tragic by-product of an unfortunate combination of biology, social circumstances, and an impulsive and neurologically immature adolescent brain that, among other causes, simply doesn't produce enough natural "feel good" neurotransmitters. The same areas of the brain responsible for feelings of happiness or sadness are involved in the process of addiction. Inadequate production and absorption of naturally occurring "feel good" neurotransmitters result in feelings of chronic sadness or anxiety. Use of substances that artificially increase availability in someone's brain of "feel good" chemicals can result in the misguided belief that the substance is the cure for their woes. For such individuals, the propensity for addiction was always there; the drugs are simply the catalyst. Individuals who do not lack the availability of these naturally occurring "feel good" neurotransmitters are not as likely to develop addiction, simply because they do not lack these chemicals and therefore do not experience the same level of neurological reward from use of the substance.

Adolescents with co-occurring disorders are too often excluded from both drug treatment clinics and from psychiatric treatment. If an adolescent with an addictive disorder seeks psychiatric care, too often their mental illness symptoms are dismissed by the provider as due to their drug abuse. The dually diagnosed adolescent is also often excluded from drug treatment centers out of the provider's ignorance. They are too often sent away from drug treatment centers until they get their mental health symptoms "stabilized"—a practice that is absolutely contraindicated by current research (SAMHSA 2011).

This practice leaves the adolescent and their families on their own, without any treatment or integrated system of care. Despite developments in the area of co-occurring disorders, individuals with a combination of substance dependency and psychological disorders seek treatment from facilities that are not willing or prepared to adequately treat them. They are often treated for one disorder without consideration of the other disorder, often "bouncing" from one type of treatment to another as symptoms of one disorder or another become predominant. Consequently, adolescents seeking treatment for substance abuse who are diagnosed with mental illness often "simply fall through the cracks and do not receive needed treatment" (Mitchell and Lawrence 2011).

Biology of Addiction

The term *genetic* refers to the biological essence of what distinguishes one person from another. Genetic information is preprogrammed and contained within our deoxyribonucleic acid (DNA). We say that genes are "expressed" by physical appearance, intelligence, and personality, for example. Although environmental factors such as nutrition, stimulation, and exposure to negative events contribute to how an individual will develop, genetics are what make our eye and hair color unique from another person. In the same manner, genetics are what determine, to a large extent, how organs are formed and whether or not there will be anomalies (deviations from the norm) in a particular organ. Just as an individual can be born with a heart that may have an anomaly resulting in a heart murmur, or another person have a pancreas that doesn't produce enough insulin and therefore develop diabetes, anomalies can occur within an individual's brain. Sometimes these neurological differences in brain structures can contribute to attention deficits, learning disorders, chronic depression, and anxiety as well as a higher risk for engaging in addictive behavior.

Attention deficit hyperactivity disorder (ADHD) is a developmental neurological disorder that is mostly resolved during late adolescence. While ADHD has no bearing on intelligence, it does indicate a longer process of brain development. Additionally, people with ADHD have difficulties not only in attention but also in impulse control and decision making as well. Due to the combination of these factors, the individual doesn't pick up on social cues as rapidly as his peers. ADHD places the adolescent at greater risk of using substances in early adolescence due to greater impulsivity and less developed social skills, which can lead to depression and a feeling of social isolation.

Unfortunately, parents and doctors became unduly influenced in the eighties and nineties by pharmaceutical company propaganda that promoted ADHD as more commonplace than it actually was. Many children who suffered from anxiety or depression were and are misdiagnosed with ADHD, also referred to as "ADD." Children who present primarily with problems of attention are more likely to have some level of depression or anxiety than their counterparts who present predominately with impulsive and hyperactive behavior (Berberich 1999). There has been much controversy regarding this topic, but it is likely that many children diagnosed with "ADD" may really have had underlying depression or anxiety that was never addressed.

The problem with so freely diagnosing children with "ADD" without a complete psychological assessment is that along with this diagnosis was an increased use of medication, which were, until fairly recently, amphetamine-based stimulants.

Stimulants increase everyone's ability to pay attention (Berberich 1999) but have an inverse effect on learning as the dosage increases. Not only is this problematic if the individual is misdiagnosed, but improper use of stimulants for an individual who does not truly have ADHD can also later lead to addiction. Additionally, children may be given medication for attention deficits instead of addressing anxiety or depression, which can be mistaken for ADHD. Consequently, their underlying depression or anxiety may never be addressed, and neither may the possible environmental stressors that contribute to their psychological state.

The growing phenomenon of medication as the first tactic applied to resolve psychological and behavioral problems rather than seeking alternative solutions seems to be connected to the ideology that medication is the cure for everything. Although medication is necessary to correct "chemical imbalances" in the brain for some people, belief of attaining instant mental health and well-being through a pill has many people looking for the "magic bullet" to fix their problems. This mindset puts too much control outside of oneself that can lead to dependence on substances rather than consideration of implementing changes in behavior and ways of seeing the world to solve all of life's problems.

A passive belief system that something external has greater control over one's behavior and thought processes is known as having an external locus of control. Conversely, when someone has an internal locus of control, that means they have the belief that they have power to change things about themselves and are not merely submissive recipients. Although it is important to understand when medication can help someone on the path to recovery, a focus on "pathology" and search for the "magic bullet" or pill to fix everything can contribute to a feeling of helplessness when things do not improve. When there is a biological basis to a disorder, medication should be an integral part of an integrated treatment plan. Even in this case, however, treatment must also address underlying thinking and social behavior that contribute to the person's negative emotional state, which can trigger anxiety, depression, or relapse.

Attention deficit hyperactivity disorder is correlated with problems of impulse control, and impulsivity contributes to addiction (Crews and Boettiger 2009). When someone has difficulties with impulsivity, they are at greater risk for developing a substance abuse disorder. Some young individuals with ADHD may also have learning disorders that slow their academic progress. When this combination occurs, a child can develop lower self-esteem. This can result in a sense of hopelessness or a sense of failure, which can lead to anxiety and depression. Unfortunately, adolescent depression is too often misinterpreted as anger and "acting out," which can stigmatize and isolate the teen, further increasing their risk of substance abuse.

Think of the brain as a system of looping and interconnected brain centers. One center activates another center, which in turn activates another. When one part of the system doesn't work properly, the other systems are affected. Impulse control is one such system that can go array if the proper "brakes" are not fully activated and therefore do not work effectively to control impulsive behavior. Neurological development occurs from the more primitive brain centers to the higher levels of brain function. The frontal lobes are the last part of the brain to develop and are not fully developed until after adolescence. Thus, adolescents do not have fully developed frontal lobes, which means impulse control, decision making, and judgment in the adolescent brain are not typically as well developed as in an adult brain.

The frontal lobes of adolescents with ADHD may take even longer to fully develop. When the frontal lobes do not fully engage, the impulse center of the brain fails to restrict behavior as it normally would. Thus, when the impulse center fails to operate, there is little to no delay between thought and action, which is the very definition of "impulsive behavior." It follows that when this neurological system fails, the individual is more likely to act without thinking, which in turn can lead to self-destructive behavior.

Individuals with impulse-control difficulties related to attention deficit hyperactivity disorder (ADHD) are often prescribed a stimulant. This stimulant works by essentially turning on the frontal lobes, which regulate impulse control, which operates the "brakes." When someone has ADHD, stimulants work in a paradoxical manner in that the person's thoughts and behavior become more regulated and slowed down.

Impulsivity can lead to addiction, in that there is less thought given in regard to use of substances. Use of potentially addictive substances lead to addiction in two primary ways: pleasure and plasticity. Pleasure refers to the stimulating effect on the reward center of the brain. Plasticity refers to the ability of certain substances to produce changes in the brain structures involved in the reward circuit from repeated use, which in turn leads to addiction (Trujillo and Molina 2007; Trujillo 2002).

A person's likelihood of developing an addiction is partly attributed to problems in impulsivity but also to the reward center of the brain (Christensen 2006). Much like other medical disorders caused by an organ that isn't functioning as effectively as it should be, addictive disorders arise from a lack of availability of dopamine in the brain. Dopamine is one of the neurotransmitters involved in feeling pleasure. Dopamine is produced and used in the reward center and controls behavior by inducing pleasurable effects. In nature, this is useful as pleasure is a great motivator and is tied to survival of the species.

Innate pleasures such as sex and food naturally induce dopamine into the reward center. However, when artificial inducers of pleasure are introduced into the brain by intoxicating substances, normal function is circumvented. The drive to obtain pleasure through natural means is slowly replaced by cravings to obtain those substances that stimulate the reward center in a more immediate and powerful way.

The drive to obtain greater and more immediate stimulation is not limited to humans. It has been demonstrated that animals can develop addictions to various substances such as cocaine. Laboratory rats will choose cocaine over food and water to the extent that they will actually starve to death, even when food is also readily available. This alone demonstrates just how powerful an addiction can be. It takes more than just willpower to pull out of the physical and psychological hold addiction has over our mind and behavior. Using involves thinking and choice, but addiction can circumvent the thinking part of our brain. In fact, the roots of addiction are controlled below our awareness and are rooted in the more primitive areas of our brain.

Addiction can also cause a change in how the brain works, moving an individual's ability to control behavior from the prefrontal cortex (the thinking part of our brain) to deeper structures in the brain: the limbic system (Everitt et al. 2008). The limbic system is a more primitive part of the brain (from an evolutionary standpoint) that controls emotion, memory, and the "reward circuit" or pleasure center (Sabatinelli et al. 2007).

Although the reward circuitry of the brain is very complex and does involve multiple neurological components, there are three primary centers in this reward circuit, the ventral tegmental area (VTA), the nucleus accumbens (Na), and the prefrontal cortex (Pc) all of which are involved in the sensation of pleasure. Two of the centers, the ventral tegmental area (VTA) and the nucleus accumbens (Na), work together as a circuit and are directly involved in addiction. The Na and VTA are connected by the median forebrain bundle (MFB), and it is this connection that becomes stronger over the course of repeatedly using addictive substances.

Normally, the prefrontal cortex (Pc) is where the signal of pleasure is sent and relays information back that acts as a braking mechanism signaling satiation, thus ending the cycle. In the process of addiction, however, this signal becomes disrupted, and the demand for stimulation to the reward center does not stop.[1]

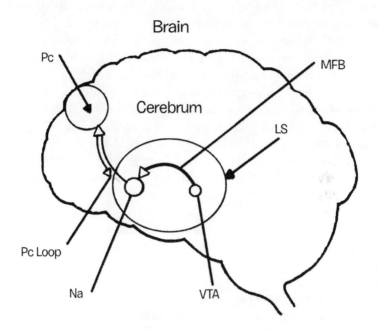

The Reward Circuit

The Reward Circuit is responsible for the sensation of pleasure and is directly involved in addiction. The *Prefrontal Cortex* (Pc) comprises the area of our brain responsible for higher levels of thinking, including decision-making, judgment, and impulse control. The Pc loop is feedback from the Pc that normally ends the reward circuit; however, repeated use of drugs and alcohol essentially shuts down this "brake," and the reward circuit becomes a stronger drive. The *limbic system* (LS) is the more primitive center of our brain and is responsible, among other things, for our mood and emotions. The *ventral tegmental area* (VTA) sends signals through the *median forebrain bundle* (MFB) to the *nucleus accumbens* (Na), which sends them to the *prefrontal cortex* (Pc). This is a simplified illustration and is not proportionally accurate. It is only intended to help graphically clarify the connections in the reward circuit.

Repeated stimulation strengthens the connection in the reward circuit between the Na and the VTA through the MFB until it becomes the sole driving force of the individual. The cycle of addiction becomes a closed loop of craving, use, euphoria (at first), withdrawal, and more craving. Over time, the drive becomes focused on obtaining the substance and becomes the predominant drive—nothing else matters.

Substances that act on this system do so essentially by increasing production of dopamine and interfering with the braking mechanism of the Pc loop. The result is behaviors that increase introductions of these substances into the system are rewarded with the initial experience of and subsequent anticipation of euphoria. Addiction to substances is so powerful that all behaviors focused on obtaining the substance begin to take priority over natural behaviors normally essential for survival, such as eating and sexual behavior. As previously mentioned, animal studies have replicated time after time that an animal will starve itself to obtain cocaine—that is how powerful substances can be.

The locus coeruleus (Lc), also involved in addiction, is activated by stress. Under stress, this center will increase the secretion of a chemical called norepinephrine, which is involved in the "fight or flight" response. People with an overactive "stress center" tend to be anxious and are more prone to being overexcited and overly emotional. Stress is a primary reason why people can relapse after an extended period of sobriety. For these individuals, the ability to tolerate stress must be learned to override their tendency toward relapse during times of increased stress.

The front area of our brain or prefrontal cortex (Pc) works as an inhibitory or "braking" mechanism for the two other areas of the reward center. Addictive substances interfere with this braking system in two ways. First, they overly stimulate the reward center of the brain, increasing its dominance and effectively increasing the limbic or emotional control over the thinking part of the brain. Second, they shut down the normal inhibitory braking effect by "numbing" the prefrontal cortex, further decreasing decision making, judgment, and impulse control. This in turn leads to a reliance on substances for immediate gratification, further strengthening the neurological dominance of the reward system and increasing its reliance on substances that increase the level of dopamine in this circuit. This results in a vicious cycle that will *always* lead to addiction.

The nucleus accumbens (Na) is the pleasure or reward center of the brain. Simply understood, the Na responds to dopamine, which is increased by things such as sex and the consumption of food and drugs.

Dopamine, a pleasure-inducing chemical, is a neurotransmitter—a chemical released into a gap between nerve cells (neurons), which allows communication between one neuron and another. Dopamine is produced in several areas of the brain, and dopamine receptors are involved in motivation, pleasure, cognition, memory, and learning.

The most fast-acting addictive substances are stimulants such as methamphetamine and cocaine, which act directly on the dopamine system in the VTA. Studies have demonstrated that certain drugs such as cocaine disrupt the normal functioning in the brain and that after withdrawal, the brain is essentially dopamine starved, taking months to regain a normal balance in the VTA (DuBois 2008). Other drugs, such as ecstasy, artificially force the release of serotonin (another neurotransmitter that is involved with feeling good), which ultimately results in a serotonin-starved brain. In some cases, normal levels of serotonin after repeated ecstasy abuse has been estimated to take years to replenish (Chudler 2003), which can result in chronic depression.

Many neurons that produce dopamine are located in the ventral tegmental area. The prefrontal cortex is also involved in this system but acts as an inhibitory mechanism. The dopamine produced in the ventral tegmental area is sent to the nucleus accumbens. For some individuals, the ventral tegmental area produces less dopamine and the nucleus accumbens is less receptive to dopamine. What this means is that the brain of someone prone toward addiction makes less dopamine and is less able to use available dopamine.

The reward center in the brain of such an individual cannot utilize dopamine as effectively as others. As a consequence, these individuals do not always feel as much pleasure nor as much happiness as others.

An individual whose brain produces and absorbs less dopamine than normal has a propensity to develop depression, depending on the environmental stressors. When a substance that acts directly on a part of the reward center[2] is introduced into their brain, that person feels happier than they are used to and interprets this as feeling "normal." The tragic irony is that the more dopamine that is artificially introduced, the more receptors are created in the reward center of the brain. At the same time, the brain is tricked into producing less dopamine than it otherwise would. The problem has now become worse as the brain requires a higher level of dopamine than it can produce on its own and at a higher level, to which it has become dependent.

---

[2]   The nucleus accumbens (Na)

Consider the mechanism of a car as a metaphor for addiction. The gas pedal is the ventral tegmental area that controls the amount of dopamine (or gas) delivered to the engine, and the brake is the prefrontal cortex. The Na could be viewed in this metaphor as the engine. If the engine isn't working efficiently, it will require more gas than it should. The VTA (gas pedal) is unable to generate enough dopamine to run the engine, so it runs at a slower speed, causing chronic depression. The more gas (dopamine) that is artificially introduced, the less efficient the engine becomes, requiring more gas to maintain its previous level of functioning.

In practice, when an individual discovers a substance such as cigarettes, caffeine, cocaine, alcohol, amphetamines, or heroin, any of which act on the reward circuit by increasing the amount of dopamine in the system, he or she will continue to use that substance due to the real and perceived immediate positive effects. Most negative physical effects (e.g., neurological damage, poor nutrition, tooth decay, collapsed veins, heart and respiratory disease) from substance abuse are typically delayed. This delay in cause and effect therefore does not negatively influence the perceived positive benefits of use, which increases repeated use and the risk of addiction.

While the substance temporarily boosts the amount of gas (dopamine) that makes it to the engine, over time, the engine becomes less efficient and requires an increasing amount for the same level of euphoria. This is tolerance. Tolerance involves both a reduced effect that the substance has on the nucleus accumbens and an increased need for the substance. What used to get someone high no longer works, and increasingly larger amounts of the substance are required to reach a previous level of euphoria, although in most cases, the original euphoric sensation is never re-experienced. This is sometimes referred to as "chasing the dragon."

Dopamine is a neurotransmitter or, more simply, a chemical messenger. Dopamine affects brain processes that include movement, mood, pleasure, and the sensation of pain. An overabundance of dopamine such as from chronic drug use results in an increase of receptors that are sensitive to this chemical messenger. However, the remaining receptors also become less sensitive to dopamine and require more of it to be stimulated. This is a process called desensitization or tolerance. Tolerance is the brain's attempt to maintain homeostasis in response to the overabundance of dopamine. It is a natural response to an unnatural state.

Logically, once this occurs, there will be an increasing demand for dopamine. This is tolerance. It's pretty simple when you break it down:

Everything that occurs from drug use is simply your brain's attempt to maintain a constant state of balance. Increased use results in less efficient receptors and a decreased ability to achieve euphoria.

The other side of addiction is withdrawal. When there is not enough dopamine in the reward center, physiological and psychological stress such as muscular cramping, nausea, pain, and anxiety increases. Once the individual stops using the substance, the brain is left high and dry and cannot yet produce enough dopamine on its own to maintain its previous level of functioning. Reduction of available dopamine results in withdrawal due to this decrease and consequent lack of available receptors from use of the drug. Once the drug is no longer introduced into the body, receptors in the nucleus accumbens will slowly go back to normal, increasing over time, and will regain their previous sensitivity to dopamine. Brain recovery such as this takes time and can be an agonizing process wrought with tremendous turmoil about whether or not to use. As Shakespeare's Hamlet so aptly put, "Aye, but there's the rub!"

Although the worst part of withdrawal passes within several days, full withdrawal involves your brain getting back to its previous level of functioning. Sleep, concentration, mood, and tolerance to pain are all worsened. The recovery process can take months to years for full normal functioning to return. It is the psychological and physiological consequences to withdrawal that typically set the individual up for relapse unless they have enough social support and acquire new cognitive skills to get through this especially challenging phase.

This process is often too unbearable for many individuals, particularly for adolescents, in the early recovery to deal with it on their own, which is the primary reason for relapse in this stage. Not only must he or she contend with withdrawal and physical pain, but as stated before, depression and anxiety also increase due to a lack of dopamine. A lack of coping skills, other than using substances to "numb" these negative moods, can be devastating and typically results in relapse during this early phase of recovery.

Adolescents in particular, due to their reliance on peer support, often experience social isolation and supreme loneliness when they are trying to get clean. They must learn to stay away from drug-using peers but are often shunned by non-using peers. There are many hurdles in recovery, and despite good intentions, most adolescents without an integrated treatment program will relapse. That is why an integrated treatment program that includes therapy, skill building, family and social support, and medication is essential for an adolescent to successfully achieve and maintain recovery.

Another factor in relapse is a process referred to as "incentive sensitization," which involves a neurological and psychological association made by an individual between anything that was involved with his or her drug use. Due to incentive sensitization, not only does the brain become physically dependent on a substance, but anything associated with that substance can also trigger a relapse.

The association of people, places, and things to one's substance abuse is referred to as "incentive stimuli" and is believed to be the underlying cause of drug craving, despite awareness of negative consequences to drug use. Due to this phenomenon, even after a long period of abstinence, just about anything remotely associated with using can trigger intense craving (Robinson 1993). Because of this process, even after an extended period of recovery, many people will relapse without ever understanding why or what caused their cravings. Therefore, an important component to therapy involves making a careful examination of everything that was involved and associated with drug use to increase personal awareness of what can trigger a craving.

Social Influences

The relationship and dynamics between an individual and his or her environment influence brain development. Our families have a stronger influence on our development when we are very young, but during adolescence, our peer group becomes a more powerful factor. Gender, race, ethnicity, and socioeconomic status also factor into the developmental process, as they can result in and influence the experiences we have during childhood and adolescence.

Family tolerance of alcohol and drug use is a powerful dynamic involved in addiction. A family history of alcohol and drug abuse increases the probability of acquiring an addiction. Drug and alcohol use by parents has been linked to an increased chance of alcohol abuse, and children of alcoholic parents are between four and eight times more likely to experience alcohol abuse than children from nonalcoholic families (Buddy 2006).

In addition to family influences, our environment has also been demonstrated to decrease or increase the probability of acquiring an addiction. "The most important precipitating factor in narcotic addiction is the degree of access to narcotic drugs" (Ausubel 1980). In the past, increased availability of drugs was thought to be a problem that belonged only to lower socioeconomic neighborhoods. Whether this was true or not, drugs are now an equal-opportunity phenomenon and have made their way in great abundance across all economic barriers. Hard-core drugs such as methamphetamine, crack cocaine, and heroin have trickled into the "middle-class" adolescent suburbia lifestyle and are fast becoming an epidemic. Heroin addiction, once considered a "ghetto drug," has now become one of the adolescent drugs of choice in suburban neighborhoods (ABC News 2008; Ausubel 1980; Frick 2011).

Another social problem that can lead to substance abuse due to feelings of hopelessness, isolation, and depression is bullying. Although bullying has been around a long time, it is only now rapidly becoming a subject of media and social interest. Cyberbullying is rapidly becoming a source of additional victimization and is also contributing to an increasing occurrence of suicide and suicide attempts (Bullying and Suicide 2013; Cyberbullying Research Summary). Bullying has recently become recognized as occurring well into adulthood in the workplace with equally devastating results on the victims (Sarver 2007).The dismissal or avoidance to intervene when a child is bullied has resulted in many victimized children succumbing to anxiety, depression, and feelings of hopelessness. Bullying ostracizes the victims, who are left isolated and therefore at greater risk for substance abuse. Hopefully, as public awareness of the destructive power of bullying increases, tolerance for bullying will decrease.

Starting in the early stage of his or her drug use, the individual will shift their friendships and associations to peers who also use. It is not uncommon for someone, during the course of addiction, to distance themselves from non-drug-using peers as well as from peers who use different drugs. There is a twisted hierarchy among substance abusers: Someone who smokes cannabis or drinks alcohol often does not see himself or herself as an addict and fails to see the similarity between themselves and others who use what they perceive to be "hard-core" drugs. Someone who uses "party drugs" such as LSD, ecstasy, cocaine, or "special K" (ketamine, also known as the "date rape drug") at social events also does not perceive him or herself as abusing drugs. Instead they see themselves as "experimenting" or just having fun.

More and more athletes and scholarly driven youth use stimulants such as methamphetamine to keep up with the increasing demands of academia, parents, and sports activities. While methamphetamine abuse is still widely prevalent, another new and dangerous trend in suburbia is smoking heroin off pieces of aluminum foil through an empty pen casing with the misconception that this method is nonaddictive. As mentioned previously, smoking or injection of a substance leads to quicker dependency on that substance than other methods of abuse.

Smoking heroin or methamphetamine is also a more expensive method of consumption as more of the substance is needed to experience the desired effects than by injection. Inevitably, due to increasing tolerance, it becomes necessary to move up to injecting to get the same euphoria initially experienced by smoking the drug. The average heroin or methamphetamine user will eventually spend $200-300 per day to support their habit. Due to this escalating cost of their growing habit, all drug users across every socioeconomic line will eventually resort to deception, stealing, or whatever it takes to support his or her habit. This is why some in the drug world refer to themselves and other long-term sufferers of addiction as "having lost their souls."

In 2010, cannabis was the most widely used illicit substance used by adolescents over the age of twelve years old. In the United States alone, over 4,476 teenagers admitted to having used cannabis (SAMHSA 2010). Although in and of itself cannabis may seem harmless to some, it truly is the "gateway" drug as it initiates the adolescent into associating with a new group of peers, many who are older and who use other "harder" substances. Access is one of the primary factors in drug usage. Involvement with a new circle of acquaintances increases access to more dangerous substances, and it is only a matter of time before the adolescent "experiments" with this broader array of drugs.

Getting high eventually becomes an activity in itself, and continued use of the substance is reinforced by acceptance into the new peer group. Non-using peers begin to distance themselves, and eventually, the only peer group available is other drug users. Deciding to stop using means more than giving up the drug; it involves giving up a lifestyle and circle of "friends." Attempts at sobriety at this point usually results in a sense of isolation due to no longer clearly fitting into any peer group. Loneliness is very often a trigger to relapse.

It is ludicrous to imagine that anyone ever plans on becoming an addict. Everyone that uses any substance starts out with the belief that they will be able to control their usage of it. This is backed up by my clinical interactions with people who have substance disorders as well as by research. "Nearly all addicted individuals believe at the outset that they can stop using drugs on their own" (NIDA 2009, 7). Once the point of tolerance is crossed over, however, there is no return to "just experimenting." With continued use, tolerance to that substance increases to the point of dependence. Recognition of dependency on a substance only occurs after withdrawal symptoms kick in during breaks in between using.

Society still generally views addiction as a choice, but it is not. Experimenting and the initial use of a substance is a choice, but with continued use, choice becomes compulsion. The compulsion to use is part of the addiction cycle and occurs earlier for some than others. How quickly someone becomes addicted to a substance is really outside of their control. "Many people do not realize that addiction is a brain disease . . . some individuals are more vulnerable than others to becoming addicted, depending on genetic makeup, age of exposure to drugs, other environmental influences and the interplay of all these factors" (NIDA 2009).

"Addiction is better defined as a behavioral syndrome where drug procurement and use seem to dominate the individual's motivation and where the normal constraints on behavior are largely ineffective" (Addiction Science Network, 2012). Although some people can limit their usage of certain substances, if an individual is predisposed toward addiction, they will most likely become dependent on that particular substance.

Depression and other psychological factors also increase the risk factor of drug use and dependency. If someone is initially attracted to using a substance to feel less anxious, depressed, or to feel "happy," it would be reasonable to assume that their brain does not produce enough of certain neurotransmitters on its own. Often the initial experiences of using result in euphoria and a reduction of negative feelings that compels the individual to use again and again. It is as though someone opens the mythical Pandora's box that, once opened, cannot be fully closed.

Pandora was a mythological Greek character. Zeus, the head Greek god, was angry that mankind had been given the gift of fire and so, in retaliation, bestowed Pandora with a gift: a beautiful container that he instructed her not to open, knowing full well that she would not be able to resist. Being human, her curiosity got the better of her. According to the myth, Pandora opened the box, allowing all forms of evil out into the world. Pandora was, however, able to close the box before everything escaped, and in this way, she was able to capture hope, the only thing left in the box. Just like for the character Pandora, hope is something that we all need. No matter how out of reach recovery may seem to be, no one ever has to give up hope because recovery is always possible.

Mental Health Factors

While drug addiction in itself is a medical and mental health disorder, a large percentage of adolescents who struggle with addiction have a coexisting mental disorder. Despite all the advances we have made as a society and improvements in a general understanding of psychology, the term "mental disorder" or "illness" still carries a negative stigma, both in the private sector and in the medical community. In regard to this very real roadblock, Steven Hyman, the director of the National Institute of Mental Health, stated, "Stigma is an important factor. Parents are fearful about bringing the social and emotional difficulties of their children to the attention of medical professionals, perhaps afraid they may be blamed. [Similarly,] children are sometimes directly stigmatized by the cruelty of classmates" (Surgeon General's Conference on Children's Mental Health 2000).

Consequently, rather than admit to having psychological problems, many adolescents suffering from depression and mood disorders often deny and try to hide their symptoms from themselves, their family, and friends. Adolescents who experiment with drugs think that certain drugs provide a temporary relief from their symptoms. What they do not realize, until perhaps it is too late, is that they have brought upon themselves a whole new set of problems. In addition to social, academic, and legal problems, substance abuse also brings about an increase in symptoms of depression, anxiety, and mental confusion and an increase in overall psychological distress.

Unfortunately, despite advances in research, there isn't enough available help from our current health care, educational, or legal systems for teens suffering from addictive or psychological disorders and certainly not when they suffer from both. Adolescents suffering from mental illness and substance abuse are not generally viewed with empathy and concern by adults in the community; rather, they are treated as problematic. They are typically excluded from any treatment, cast out of the mainstream educational system, and too often land headfirst into our criminal justice system.

Despite what looks and sounds good on paper about the theory of "rehabilitation," funding for any real rehabilitation has been drastically cut. Once involved with the legal system, it is more likely an adolescent will simply fall further and further down the rabbit hole. Ties with their family, friends, and the positive mainstream community are increasingly replaced with connections to individuals in the criminal and drug subcultures.

Although researchers are still arguing about whether drug abuse causes mental illness or if it is the other way around, it is likely that both occur, as previously discussed, as a result of the same built-in neurological factors. Additionally, drug abuse clearly increases psychological and cognitive problems and an exacerbation of psychiatric symptoms. In addition to other research, the National Institute of Mental Health and Johns Hopkins have been researching bipolar disorder and possible genetic variables involved. Although there is yet no conclusive evidence about whether bipolar disorder can be caused by drug abuse, it has been determined that the symptoms of and treatment for mood disorders that are diagnosed before or after drug use are essentially the same.

There is growing verification that genetic variables are involved with addiction. While it has been established that bipolar disorder is genetically passed down through family members, the specific genes involved are still a mystery. In a collaborative effort sponsored by the National Institute of Mental Health (NIMH) and Johns Hopkins Medicine Psychiatry and Behavioral Sciences Mood Disorders Center, research is being conducted to determine the specific genes responsible for bipolar disorder (Johns Hopkins 2012).

As previously mentioned, the same brain structures involved with affective disorders (depression and mood disorders) are involved with addiction. Individuals who suffer from a mental illness are twice as likely to abuse substances. Individuals with co-occurring mental and substance abuse disorders are also more likely to suffer from more severe psychiatric symptoms (National Institute on Drug Abuse, National Institute of Health, and the US Department of Health and Human Services 2010) and feelings of hopelessness. The tragic combination of depression and impulsivity associated with being under the influence of a substance can create the perfect storm, leading to suicidal thoughts and resulting in a spontaneous decision that has permanent and deadly consequences.

Bipolar disorder is perhaps the most overdiagnosed and, ironically, most misunderstood of mental disorders that affect adolescents. Many adolescents with an addictive disorder and bipolar disorder fall through the cracks as their behaviors are often written off as due to emotional problems associated with adolescence and with drug use. However, bipolar disorder is not a lightweight problem and, if not correctly treated, can have fatal consequences. One out of three adolescent males who are diagnosed with bipolar disorder will die by suicide before their twenty-fifth birthday. Suicide is the fourth leading cause of death in the United States for adults aged eighteen to twenty-five, surpassing other causes of death, including diabetes, stroke, and homicide (SAMHSA 2010; NIMH 2007).

Due to severity of potential consequences if left untreated, depressive and mood disorders should be considered as a "rule out" during the initial assessment of a co-occurring disorder. Bipolar disorder involves unpredictable and sometimes severe shifts in mood. It is very likely that a large percentage of individuals suffering from addiction also suffer from depression or bipolar disorder.

Adolescents and young adults with bipolar disorder are typically passionate and impulsive and, without medication to stabilize their psychiatric symptoms, will seek out the quickest means such as substance abuse to reduce unbearable symptoms of agitation, anxiety, irritability, rage, insomnia, and severe depression. It is crucial to identify early treatment if there is a mood disorder, as medication to stabilize psychiatric symptoms is paramount for sustained and successful recovery.

Given all these factors, there is a compelling need for treatment of adolescents with co-occurring disorders of addiction and mental illness. The level of contribution drug abuse can have on mental illness is still not clear, although certainly many individuals suffering from mental illness have turned to substance abuse as an attempt to manage or self-medicate their symptoms. What is clear is that adolescents who are suffering from both disorders are in desperate need of help. They need immediate and effective treatment to reduce their potential risk of suicide and to help them live a more meaningful and happier life. Despite this compelling need, most treatment centers do not effectively address, diagnose, or treat comorbid mental illness and substance abuse disorders for adolescents.

Treatment Exclusion

There are many differing viewpoints as to what substance abuse treatment should entail. Co-occurring mental health disorders are not typically addressed in standard drug counseling. As discussed earlier, there are substantial roadblocks for adolescents who have co-occurring mental health and substance abuse disorders to receive treatment that addresses both disorders at the same time. Too often, individuals with co-occurring disorders are excluded from receiving any mental health or substance abuse treatment. Both drug counselors and mental health providers too often fail to see or treat the adolescent as suffering from two distinct but interconnected disorders. This practice is based on ignorance of what co-occurring disorders are and a lack of adequate training in this area of mental health treatment. The result to this outdated practice is adolescents and their families are typically frustrated and discouraged from receiving treatment. If they are fortunate enough to obtain any treatment, most available treatment is generally inadequate and equally discouraging as mental health and substance abuse disorders are not adequately or equally addressed.

There is an expectation by many drug counselors that the adolescent must get their mental health disorder stabilized before that provider will provide treatment for substance abuse. Additionally, many drug counselors are not adequately trained to recognize or address psychiatric disorders. Likewise, many mental health providers tend to stigmatize addiction and have the opinion that the substance abuse disorder must first be resolved before the individual can benefit from therapy or treatment. There is also a hesitation by mental health providers to treat adolescents suffering from co-occurring disorders based on the erroneous belief that addiction is the primary problem and psychiatric symptoms are a result of substance abuse and will resolve once drug use stops.

Despite this current practice of splitting and denying treatment, there are effective methods to treatment for adolescents with co-occurring disorders. Inpatient treatment is perhaps the ideal treatment of severe co-occurring disorders but is impractical and financially out of reach for most. Alternatively, the National Institute on Drug Abuse (NIDA) recommends intensive day treatment in an outpatient program as "more suitable for people with jobs or extensive social supports" than residential or inpatient treatment. The NIDA advised against "low-intensity" programs as they may "offer little more than drug education" (NIDA 2008). To address treatment inconsistencies and to improve treatment outcomes, SAMHSA's Co-occurring Center for Excellence calls for "evidence-based treatment" (SAMHSA and Center for Mental Health Services, Center for Substance Abuse Treatment 2007). This approach entails utilization of available research, theory, practices, guidelines, clinical experience, and training to arrive at a method of practice that has a stronger likelihood of a successful outcome to treatment. A review of a broad spectrum of evidence-based research found consensus as to the most effective drug treatment program.

Integration of Treatment

The most successful outcomes for drug treatment appear to be a multimodal approach. This approach includes individual and group cognitive behavioral therapy, awareness, and problem solving, skill building, group peer support, family therapy, psychopharmacological interventions by psychiatrists and addiction specialists to stabilize psychological distress and symptoms, and ongoing involvement in group therapy or 12-step programs. Other components to treatment may include identifying additional needed resources such as housing and coordination with other involved agencies (education, social services, or legal) with terms agreed upon at the start of treatment by the adolescent and his or her family so as to not violate confidentiality and trust.

Substance Abuse and Mental Health Services Administration (SAMHSA) identifies additional guiding principles for working with individuals who have mental health and substance abuse disorders (SAMHSA, Center for Mental Health Services, Center for Substance Abuse Treatment 2007). Among these principles is the recognition that recovery is a long-term process that involves setting task-specific treatment goals to address this process. Ideal treatment goals should incorporate the multiple collateral issues involved, including medical, mental health, educational, occupational, family, and social concerns, in addition to mental health and substance abuse concerns. Possible temporary or chronic functional or cognitive issues as a result of substance abuse may also need to be addressed in treatment planning. Lastly, treatment goals need to address building long-term support, including family and other community support systems, as part of the continuity of care necessary to sustain stability and sobriety.

Integrated treatment of co-occurring disorders has been demonstrated to be more effective than most currently available community-based treatments (NIDA 2008). Currently, typical community-based treatment does not integrate mental illness with substance abuse disorders. Individuals suffering from co-occurring disorders are unlikely to get treatment for both disorders from the same provider and are expected to get one of their disorders stabilized before the other will be addressed. In short, the current mainstream manner of treatment does not adequately address the treatment needs for an individual with a co-occurring disorder.

This current practice of essentially splitting treatment or exclusion from treatment has resulted in a high relapse rate and places the adolescent at high risk of suicide due to feelings of hopelessness. Suicide is one of the highest causes of death for adolescent males (NIH and National Institute on Drug Abuse, 2004). This risk is much higher when adolescents are suffering from co-occurring disorders. Adolescents who present with one disorder are more likely to suffer from co-occurring disorders than not (Arcelus and Vostanis 2005; NIH and National Institute on Drug Abuse, 2004).

Integrated treatment is the active, simultaneous treatment of psychological issues and substance abuse and involves drug and relapse prevention education, coping, skills building, motivational and cognitive behavioral psychotherapy, group therapy, family therapy, and psychiatry. An integrated treatment program utilizes a combination of therapy modalities, which can include drug and relapse prevention concepts and skills, motivational interviewing, cognitive behavioral techniques, meditation and mindfulness training, family therapy, peer support, and other types of group therapy. Coordination with addiction specialists, psychiatry, outside community support systems, and continued support through alumni young-adult group and family support groups are also recommended as part of an integrated treatment approach.

Another obstacle to maintained sobriety is the practice of imposing preordained time limitations to treatment. Frequently, outpatient treatment time limitations are based on insurance guidelines rather than clinical considerations or clinical research and do not generally provide an ideal length of treatment. Access to care in an integrated system needs to be based on a more realistic time frame as well as to incorporate flexibility and ongoing assessment of individual needs rather than a predetermined "one size fits all" length of treatment.

After the primary treatment goals have been met, secondary long-term goals to maintain recovery need to be established. Eventually, clinical therapeutic needs are slowly phased out with continuation of supportive peer-based groups and coordination of any continued psychiatric treatment needs. General supportive systems such as peer support and individual therapy can be offered as long as they are needed for the individual to maintain their psychological well-being and sobriety. During and after treatment, the individual should continue their relationship with community-based 12-step programs. Hopefully, during this period of time, they have also been developing new and healthier relationships as well to replace the more toxic associations they have moved away from.

Aftercare should continue after the adolescent becomes stabilized and acclimated to their new lifestyle. Premature termination of treatment jeopardizes sobriety as adolescents without a solid support system in place are at risk for feeling isolated and therefore are at greater risk of relapse.

Termination of treatment cannot be based on a concrete and preordained time period. A more successful treatment outcome is achieved when the individual is doing well enough on his or her own for an extended period of time past physical and psychological recovery and has learned enough cognitive skills to cope with periods of stress. Continued access to support systems such as 12-step or other forms of support programs are important components to continued success and sobriety as well as having a plan of what to do and who to call to access support if relapse does occur.

PART FOUR

Method in the Madness

Treatment of Adolescents with Co-occurring Disorders

The following is a brief overview of evidence-based treatment to be provided in an intensive day-treatment center. Treatment is based on the research, experience, and wisdom of leaders in the field of psychology and drug treatment. The concepts may not seem to fit together, but there is "method to the madness" (Shakespeare) in the complex treatment of co-occurring disorders. Each aspect of treatment is like a piece in a puzzle; all build upon one another. The pieces of the puzzle include screening, evaluation and treatment planning, drug education, relapse prevention, motivational interviewing, cognitive therapy, coping and conflict resolution skills, awareness training, group therapy, family therapy, medication management and coordination with psychiatric and addictive medicine providers, educational and occupational planning, aftercare, and coordination with access to community support systems.

Prior to receiving treatment, the overall functioning and needs of the individual must be assessed. According to research (SAMHSA 2011), the level of severity of mental illness and substance dependency can be assigned into four quadrants (p. 62) or levels that will help clarify the specific level of treatment the individual needs to begin their recovery. The first level of care is assigned to those individuals identified with less severe mental health and substance disorders. This level is for adolescents identified as having milder psychological concerns and who are abusing substances but may not yet suffer from addiction.

At this level, the adolescent may be successfully treated by outpatient drug counseling and therapy. The needs for such an individual may be resolved within several months and with less intensive treatment, typically meeting several times per week with both a therapist and a drug counselor.

The second level of treatment is assigned to individuals with less severe substance disorders but who have more severe mental health challenges. The third level includes individuals who suffer from less severe mental health disorders and more severe substance disorders. Both of these levels are considered moderate and, in some instances, may require short-term stabilization in an inpatient setting. Adolescents assessed at the more severe fourth level of treatment needs are those who suffer from severe mental health and addictive disorders and most likely require placement in an inpatient facility for detoxification and stabilization before they can be treated successfully in an intensive day-treatment setting.

An intensive outpatient day-treatment center level of care has been determined to be as beneficial as inpatient settings for most individuals who meet criteria for levels two and three (SAMHSA 2011). An integrated intensive day-treatment center treats the entire individual and their co-occurring mental health and substance disorders simultaneously. In this system of care, mental health and addictive disorders are simultaneously addressed and treated; there is no waiting for one to be in remission before addressing the other.

The theory is simple. For individuals who have co-occurring disorders, one disorder cannot be treated successfully without treating the other at the same time. Most important to this treatment concept is that addiction is seen more as a symptom of a mental disorder than a separate and unrelated disorder. In this model of care, addiction is not treated without addressing the underlying emotional, psychological, and physiological factors that the individual has been unsuccessfully attempting to "self-medicate."

Screening and Evaluation

Treatment begins at intake with an initial screening. Ideally, screening should occur after some level of trust and rapport is established, to increase openness in behalf of the client. At this stage it is important to assess the length, frequency, and severity of substance abuse. It is also vital to evaluate the individual for any serious mental health concerns and risk of self-harm. Lastly, a sense of the client's actual willingness and readiness for treatment should be determined.

The primary purpose of screening is to gather a working concept of the adolescent and his or her family members' immediate and most serious concerns. Although treatment for addictive and mental health disorders is equally important, immediate screening for the degree of substance abuse is of primary importance at the onset of treatment. Since substance abuse directly impacts psychiatric symptoms and current functioning, it is necessary to know what the adolescent has been using and how severe their level of substance abuse is. A more thorough assessment of the adolescent will take place over an extended period of time to determine the extent other factors such as a psychiatric symptoms, personality, cognitive processes, family dynamics, and peer influences need to be addressed in treatment.

The initial intake assessment involves one or more self-report checklists, a clinical interview, and an observation of symptoms and behavior that may indicate if the adolescent is presently under the influence or experiencing withdrawal from a substance. There are several screening tools routinely used to assess the presence and severity of addiction. One of these tools is the Simple Screening Instrument for

Substance Abuse or SSI-SA, which has been widely used and validated as a reliable instrument for the adolescent population (Center for Substance Abuse Treatment 1994).

Screening is useful in determining the reported extent of substance abuse as well as to gather a quick picture of co-occurring mental health concerns. Unless the individual is suffering from severity of symptoms warranting immediate medical treatment, supportive and motivational therapy can begin during the first session. If there is a need for medical intervention to address severe withdrawal symptoms or psychiatric instability, a means to access immediate emergency care needs to be facilitated and not just left to the individual and his or her family to figure out on their own.

The clinical evaluation focuses on reported and observed symptoms and behaviors that may reveal depression, anxiety, mood disorders, and possible thought or perceptual disturbances in addition to substance abuse. If the focus of the initial evaluation is only on behavioral issues or substance abuse, underlying mental health symptoms may be minimized or entirely missed. It is unlikely that a full disclosure will come about initially. An important goal during the first contact is to establish trust and to compel the adolescent to be as forthcoming as possible. Establishing trust and mutual respect are the key components to successful treatment because without it, it is unlikely that the adolescent would be willing to discuss in depth their symptoms and certainly not the full extent of their drug abuse. With each contact, the therapist will have more information available from disclosures and their own clinical observations to more accurately narrow down individualized treatment needs.

Although parental consent is required unless certain conditions are met, effective treatment has been demonstrated to require a more passive stance on behalf of the parents. A passive involvement means support from parents or caretakers and a willingness to respect information the adolescent exchanges with the therapist as confidential. This is not to collude with the adolescent or to split them from their family but to establish an agreed-upon level of confidentiality. This increases the likelihood of genuine participation by the adolescent in their treatment and a more successful outcome of treatment. If he or she confides in the therapist and this confidence is broken, treatment will come to a grinding halt. Therefore, it is part of the initial session to meet with both the teen and his or her parent to explain how confidentiality works, to not have any misunderstandings or subsequent sabotage of treatment.

The family can be offered the opportunity to participate in treatment by providing their perspective during a parent interview and attending subsequent family sessions. All family members' patterns of interacting with each other are evaluated and addressed during family sessions. Family therapy does not single out the teen as "the identified patient." Any dysfunctional family dynamics, which may have contributed to the teen's current situation and that may later interfere with his or her recovery, are primary areas of focus during these sessions. However, although all family members are held accountable for their behavior, the primary function of family therapy is not a time for placing blame but is proactive and holds a positive problem-solving stance. Emotional support from family members is vital. Parents and siblings can provide support for the adolescent by participating in family therapy with the goal of reducing tension and improving the bond between family members.

A quick note at this point is in regard to adolescents and young adults who refuse to participate in any treatment. One solution for adolescents is that they can be placed into an inpatient facility to detox or to stabilize psychiatric symptoms and, upon their release, be brought to a day treatment center for help, using whatever leverage a parent might have. Sadly, unless drastic legal action is taken, our system removes parental legal authority and power once a minor turns eighteen. Until this is changed, it is all the more reason to address co-occurring disorders as soon and as early as possible.

Stages of Recovery

It is more likely than not that the adolescent is not fully motivated at the onset of treatment to fully participate nor is it likely that they are fully aware of their need for treatment. Prochaska and DiClemente developed a method that assesses an individual's level of awareness and acceptance of having an addiction as well as of their motivation for recovery. This system is called the transtheoretical model, and it identifies five progressive stages of change in regard to acceptance of the need to change. The theoretical stages of change in this model are referred to as precontemplation, contemplation, preparation, maintenance, and relapse (DiClemente and Prochaska 1982; Prochaska and DiClemente 1982).

This theory proposes that during addiction and recovery, an individual will move between the different stages and that assessment and recognition of what stage the individual is in throughout treatment is essential. Equally important in this model is developing an adaptable and appropriate treatment plan to adjust for the individual's movement in and out of the different stages of recovery. Flexibility of a treatment plan is required so that treatment conforms to individual needs with the understanding that movement between stages is not necessarily achieved in a predictable or linear manner. It is important to note that relapse is considered one of the stages of recovery and is not evidence of failed treatment but a predictable aspect of the process of recovery.

Change can be hard, and arriving at a point where one is aware of the need for change on his or her own may not occur in time to prevent serious negative consequences. Adolescence is an important developmental period of growth, which increases the urgency of initiating treatment. Treatment of adults requires full consent, but with adolescents, parents can make the choice to begin treatment. Although getting an adolescent into treatment does not guarantee cooperation or instant success, it is a start, and the alternative can be and, most likely will be, a tragic loss.

The precontemplation stage is before the individual has awareness that there is a problem and therefore requires sensitivity on behalf of the therapist to gain a level of trust, which will encourage both participation and willingness to return to the next session. At this point, the adolescent most likely has not yet made the connection of how much their substance abuse has negatively impacted their life. It is usually the family or other people in his or her life who are aware of current and potential consequences and who usually initiate treatment.

In many regards, this is the most difficult stage of treatment. This is the stage where negative consequences from substance abuse have not yet tipped the adolescent's sense of balance of gain versus risk. Using is still viewed by the adolescent as a viable escape from negative mood states or circumstances without any obvious alternatives or consequences. Even when someone has ambivalence about using, they are not always aware that it has moved past free choice to dependency.

The contemplative stage is when the adolescent is starting to be aware that he may have a problem. The balance is beginning to shift due to the realization that there are now more negative than positive experiences from using. Despite this shift, he has not yet been able to fully admit that he is addicted. This is still the stage of denial.

Drug education about the biological components and long-term consequences of addiction is important during this stage and may encourage motivation to participate in treatment. Education about the social and psychological components underlying substance abuse may help to encourage participation in treatment. Learning to recognize the symptoms of depression, anxiety, and mood disorders and ways in which they can be lessened without using may decrease an adolescent's feelings of isolation and despair.

The true beginning of treatment is the engagement stage, and it is at this point that the individual becomes more willing to participate. During this stage, there is a shift in perception about addiction and a reduction in the level of resistance. In addition to a shift in perspective, this stage cannot be achieved unless trust is established. One of the roadblocks to developing trust may be prior negative experiences with authority figures and previous misguided therapists.

A previous negative experience with a therapist who was unsuitably trained, emotionally distant, or otherwise unresponsive to the adolescent's needs creates a serious barrier to future treatment that must be addressed and overcome. Especially if this has occurred, rapport and trust cannot be rushed. Patience, genuineness, and sensitivity on behalf of the therapist are necessary components to successfully engaging the teen in active participation in their recovery. Adolescents are typically sharper and more intuitive than given credit by most adults and can sense when a therapist is not sincere. Only a therapist who is well trained and passionate about his or her work will have the ability, energy, enthusiasm, and credibility to be able to successfully engage an adolescent in therapy.

The preparation stage is marked by the adolescent becoming aware of and accepting the need to change. At this stage, therapy can help guide the client to identify his or her goals. In addition to individual therapy, group therapy can provide further validation for what the adolescent has been going through as well as provide important emotional support through peer approval for his or her decision to change.

When a decision to change is made, active involvement toward establishing and achieving sobriety begins. Maintenance is achieved after a period of time during which an observable commitment to sobriety has been established. As recovery is a process, there may be movement back and forth between stages. Relapse can occur during this time and must be addressed without critical input to encourage return to sobriety. It is unlikely once progress has been made past the stage of denial that the individual will ever fall back into full denial even if they have relapsed. Some slipping backward, as in relapse, is not an indication of failure; it is time to take a step back and see what is going on in the individual's life and where more focus is needed. A more positive way to see relapse is that the individual is still a "work in progress" and that this process is not always smooth and predictable. Every person is unique, and so is their recovery process, which is likely to present different challenges from other people's experiences.

Stress is one of the major triggers to relapse. Relapse prevention, therefore, involves learning new ways to handle stress as well as pinpointing other triggers to relapse. Coping skills to deal with stress are taught and practiced through various therapeutic methods, including mindfulness training and cognitive behavioral therapy, both having been researched and validated as useful in the treatment of bipolar disorder (United States Department of Veteran Affairs, 2010). It is also important to improve social skills and to learn ways to resolve interpersonal conflicts through group and family therapy. Additionally, coordination with outside agencies—which may provide additional support such as medical care, housing, educational, and occupational assistance—may also be important collateral components of treatment in the recovery process.

Advocating for the adolescent with outside agencies such as social services or probation may be necessary as part of the integration of care. Working with outside agencies to resolve real-life difficulties that may have resulted from the previous activities involved with substance abuse is part of the coordination of care. Encouraging and helping the adolescent to identify life goals and to successfully engage with the community, such as completion of high school and enrolling in vocational training or college, will also increase self-esteem and motivation in achieving other long-term goals. Establishment of long-term goals will help the adolescent become more self-sufficient and successful in achieving their aspirations in life so as to foster a greater sense of self-worth, hope, and motivation to remain in recovery.

Education and Relapse Prevention

The early phase of treatment should provide the adolescent and their family with knowledge and understanding of addiction and, minimally, the interaction between environmental stressors, psychological disorders, and drug addiction. Education-based individual or group sessions that address the biological, psychological, and social components of addiction and the recovery process should be made available to the adolescent and his or her family. The goal of drug education is to help families to understand not only the short- and long-term effects of different substances on the brain and body but to increase their ability to recognize the early signs of relapse. Adolescents who are in the early stages of recovery need to be aware of the unseen physiological consequences of addiction. An additional goal of therapy therefore is to help the individual develop a greater awareness of the long-term physical consequences of addiction to their physical well-being and overall health to increase his or her motivation to establish and to maintain sobriety.

For individuals suffering from co-occurring disorders, full recovery necessitates addressing addictive and mental health factors. There are many negative misconceptions about mental illness, and the stigma attached to mental illness prevents many who suffer from co-occurring disorders from seeking treatment for their psychiatric symptoms.

Out of desperation and a lack of knowledge, many teens turn to self-medication with whatever substance that provides them with an immediate and illusory escape from emotional pain. Understanding the dynamic and interactional role of substances on mental illness is instrumental in the recovery process. Increased understanding about mental illness and the painful emotional suffering an adolescent is going through also improves understanding, compassion, and support for the adolescent by their families, which will increase available emotional support and in the recovery process as well.

The disease model—which is used for medical disorders such as diabetes, high blood pressure, and other chronic disorders—can be applied to the treatment of addictive and mental health disorders. Without an integrated system of care in the treatment of addiction, the prognosis for recovery is poor. Addiction is a progressive and ultimately chronic disorder that can result in increasing loss of everyday functioning and is, in fact, a slow death. The adolescent and their family need to understand the importance of applying this conceptualization of a chronic medical disorder to addiction to support and maintain a more successful recovery.

In this model, treatment of symptoms of a co-occurring disorder and compliance to recommended treatment is similar to treatment of other chronic medical disorders. This recovery model utilizes the concept of constant progress toward recovery, even if the patient is noncompliant to treatment and relapse occurs.

As discussed earlier, a return of symptoms due to noncompliance in the treatment of chronic disorders is not considered a failure. Any period of time in which there is a reduction of symptoms (in the treatment of addiction, this means not using) is considered progress. Treatment of addiction should be approached in the same manner.

If someone diagnosed with a chronic medical disorder such as diabetes is inconsistent and noncompliant in their medication regime, efforts are made to improve their compliance to treatment with the aim of establishing a greater response to treatment. Similarly, in the treatment of addiction, relapse is due to some level of noncompliance with treatment. Relapse essentially involves a return of symptoms.

Comparable to other chronic disorders, this is cause for a reexamination of individual treatment needs and is not an indication of treatment failure. In this model of treatment and recovery, there is no failure, only progress toward the reduction and ultimate elimination of the symptoms of addiction.

Motivation for Change

Most methods that address substance abuse, including supportive systems such as 12-step programs, only work if and when an individual wants to stop their downward spiral. Getting someone into treatment when they do not want help can be a start, but a clear understanding of where that person stands in regard to accepting help can determine whether treatment will be successful over time. Addressing the individual's stage of recovery and motivation for change, therefore, needs to be part of the initial assessment as well as a continuing process throughout treatment. The key word here is "motivation"—knowing whether the person is actually at a point where they want help and will take treatment seriously must be ascertained. When someone is not ready to accept help, the approach must be supportive, not confrontational. Support can be simply listening to what is going on in their life and gaining enough trust for them to share their emotions and life situation.

Miller and Rollnick (Miller, W. and Rollnick, S.,1991) developed a fresh approach to eliciting change within an individual and termed this method "motivational interviewing." Much of their concept stems from the work of Carl Rogers (1951) and his theory of the necessary conditions for real change to occur during the course of a therapeutic relationship. Motivational interviewing is most useful when the individual is stuck and not yet committed to change. It is not a therapy, technique, or "something to be done to people to make them change" (Naar-King and Suarez 2011). Motivational interviewing is a client-centered therapeutic style, not a collection of techniques, and is directed at reducing the adolescent's ambivalence about their substance abuse. "Motivational interviewing is a collaborative, person centered form of guiding to elicit and strengthen motivation for change" (Miller and Rollnick 2009). The core concept of this approach is helping the client to arrive at their own conclusion regarding their addictive behavior and a personal decision to achieve sobriety.

The goal of this process is not to provide advice or challenge how someone thinks and feels. The primary purpose of treatment at this stage is to help the adolescent come to a point where they can begin to develop a personal reason for change and decide to change for intrinsic and personally meaningful reasons rather than to appease other people in their life. The process of lasting recovery begins as a cognitive shift of cause and effect. Ultimately, power to change comes from within.

During the recovery process, a new sense of self and personal goals will develop as well as increased self-control. From this, a better decision-making process will develop with an increased, internally motivated desire to work toward sobriety. In psychology, we call this an internal versus external locus of control. More simply put, one needs to develop a self-driven and self-motivated system of reasons, goals, and desires to change.

A popular but tragic musician's fateful song lyrics about refusing to go to rehabilitation reflect the reality of how fruitless it is to try to force someone to change. With most people, and especially adolescents, any perceived attempt to coerce or manipulate them will only push them further away, even if, at some level, they want help. Adolescence and young adulthood is a period during which there is a tremendous psychological need to achieve autonomy and a more complete and genuine sense of self. The desire to change must be self-generated and motivated; any attempt to change for the sake of appeasing someone other than one's self is less likely to be sustained.

Motivational interviewing was developed initially for working with adults who had substance abuse disorders. There is strong evidence that motivational interviewing is an important and recommended part of integrated care (NIDA 2009; Center for Substance Abuse Treatment 1999). This approach is more of a pretreatment approach than therapy. It has the purpose of guiding the individual to see for himself or herself how their substance abuse has been problematic and the benefits to moving away from dependency on substances. Although the implementation of this method of engagement for the treatment of adolescent substance abuse is relatively new compared to its use in adult populations, there is increasing evidence that it improves treatment outcome (Hettema et al. 2005).

Cognitive Therapy

Ironically, research has demonstrated that people who have a tendency toward depressive and negative thoughts may have better reality testing than other people. Depression is thought by some to have a possible evolutionary purpose as it may increase analytic and problem solving thought (Andrews and Thomson 2009). However, as ruminating thoughts escalate into depression, reality testing goes out the window. Irrational and exaggerated negative thoughts not based on real events further escalate anxiety and depression until reality testing is replaced by catastrophic and hopeless thoughts that degrade the already fragile sense of self-worth. Individuals who are prone to depression and anxiety must switch from their dysfunctional approach of dealing with problems to a more positive and rational way of problem solving.

Cognitive behavioral therapy was developed by Aaron Beck in the 1960s (Beck et al. 1979). A dysfunctional system of thoughts and beliefs is referred to in cognitive therapy as cognitive distortions. "Cognitive" refers to how we think, and cognitive distortions are exaggerated, emotionally based, and irrational thoughts that foster misinterpretations of events and other people's intentions. This type of thinking is not based on reality but on an emotionally charged way of interpreting or seeing events. Think of distorted thinking similar to a fun house mirror, which reflects your body image in a distorted manner; it is not reflective of reality but is an illusion.

Cognitive therapy helps an individual identify their unique system of thoughts and any thought distortions. Automatic negative and distorted thoughts are what drive anxious, depressed, and hopeless feelings. This method of teaching people how to think more rationally is useful in the treatment of addiction in conjunction with other therapeutic methods as it addresses underlying patterns of thinking that can lead to cravings and substance abuse (Beck et al. 1993).

Cognitive therapy is a fact-finding and problem-solving intervention. It doesn't seek to uncover mysterious, "subconscious," or trauma-based reasons behind substance abuse. The goal of this therapeutic method is more observable and direct so as to "reduce excessive emotional reactions and self-defeating behavior by modifying faulty or erroneous thinking and maladaptive beliefs that underlie these reactions" (Beck et al. 1993, 27). More simply put, the individual learns to identify their own faulty thinking patterns and starts to adjust their thoughts from being emotionally based to reality based.

Automatic thoughts are simply rapid thoughts that occur below our direct awareness. Negative and distorted automatic thoughts result in a negative, depressed, or anxious response to an event usually without any basis in reality. Many of these thoughts stem from dysfunctional and perhaps abusive interpersonal experiences from earlier in life and have outlived their usefulness. Negative automatic thoughts impair one's perception of events and drive emotional and reactive behavior. Such thoughts are often the core of sudden cravings, relapse, and feelings of hopelessness.

Distorted thinking drives negative belief systems, which in turn affect how we act in relation to a neutral or positive event that is erroneously interpreted as a negative event. A tendency to see things negatively, in turn, impacts our interactions with others and perception of events. We think things are worse than they really are. The end result is that our negative perception of an event results in our negative behavior and typically elicits a negative response from the environment (others). It is a vicious cycle, making life experiences progressively worse.

There are many types of negative and distorted thinking, including catastrophizing, overgeneralizing, magnifying, polarizing, and filtering. Catastrophizing is just as it sounds. Events are perceived as all or none without any factual basis and with the most negative, extreme consequences imaginable. You walk by a friend and say hello, but they don't respond. If you fall victim to your own tendency to catastrophize, you may think that they didn't respond because they hate you and that your friendship is over. When you learn how to challenge your negative distorted thoughts, you may instead think that he or she was deep in thought, is still your friend, and may simply have not seen nor heard you.

A major focus in cognitive behavioral therapy is on changing negative cognitions (automatic thoughts) and belief systems (life perspective). In the treatment of addiction, cognitive therapy is used to identify personal patterns of thinking that contribute to addictive behavior. Cognitive therapy focuses on identifying automatic thoughts as well as irrational, idiosyncratic, and dysfunctional beliefs, all of which contribute to emotional distress and can trigger a relapse. Through the course of therapy, dysfunctional thoughts are slowly replaced with more rational and optimistic problem-solving strategies to reduce stress and negative mood states, ultimately reducing stress and the risk of relapse.

Substance abuse interferes with the acquisition of important cognitive and behavioral skills due to the immediate interference of the substance on natural cognitive and emotional responses to an event. Rather than learning how to resolve a conflict by thinking things through, the individual develops a reliance on mind-altering substances to emotionally numb out and never acquires fundamental cognitive strategies or skills to self-calm. The individual uses substances to escape from their emotional state and never develops skills to resolve stress and emotional pain. To achieve and maintain recovery, a new system of problem-solving skills therefore must be part of treatment to replace substance dependency as self-medication, or the individual will fall back to old ways to escape from unexpected stress and painful events.

Cognitive restructuring is a therapy technique that teaches how to recognize and challenge irrational and self-defeating thoughts. Sometimes irrational thoughts are so fast that they fall below the radar. Even though these thoughts can create a shift in one's emotional state, they are not easily noticed. The individual learns how to pay attention to their thoughts and to sort out what is reality based, what is not, and how this pattern of thinking can increase anxiety or depression and trigger relapse.

In combination with psychopharmacological medication, cognitive therapy is very effective in the treatment of depression. Regardless of how the distorted and self-destructive thoughts developed, there is no point in assigning blame. This type of therapy is focused on problem solving and is future focused with an emphasis on developing a realistic set of ideas and learning to dismiss thoughts that have no real basis.

Cognitive behavioral therapy is used in relapse prevention treatment as it increases an individual's ability to identify triggers to relapse—such as high-risk situations, people, and places—and coping strategies to use should these situations arise. Over time, with effort and acceptance of feedback during individual and group therapy, the adolescent can develop a more positive manner of thinking and reacting to his or her automatic thoughts. Cognitive therapy is also used to identify situations that hold a high risk for relapse and to develop thoughts called "control beliefs" that can help counteract high-risk situations. Control beliefs include such thoughts as "I can cope without using" or "I don't need drugs to have fun," "A lapse is not equivalent to failure," "Even if I slip, I don't have to continue using drugs"—all of which "counter" and dispel thoughts that could otherwise lead to relapse (Beck et al. 1993, 299).

Addiction has a domino effect. Over time, the individual becomes increasingly reliant on the substance due to his or her belief that it is the only way to resolve pain. This in turn leads to more collateral problems from substance use but keeps the individual locked in. They continue to use despite problems caused by using, as the substance temporarily ends emotional and physical pain. In the broad field of science known as behaviorism, this is called negative reinforcement. Use of substances appears to remove bad emotional or physical feelings. This in turn reinforces using the substance because it is now associated with the cessation of those bad feelings. Although use of an intoxicating or numbing substance may temporarily remove emotional pain, over time, increasing amounts of the substance become necessary to achieve this same state until constant use is necessary just to maintain a "normal" mood and avoid withdrawal symptoms. The goal, once addicted, is no longer to achieve "euphoria"; although the individual may fool themselves into believing this, it is to avoid the pain of withdrawal. This is what is meant by developing a tolerance to the substance or "chasing the dragon."

Drug education increases understanding of the process of addiction, and this understanding can help someone take a step back and look at what is really going on rather than to continue to live in denial. Knowledge is power and is essential for successful recovery. Understanding the actual physical changes that occur in the brain due to substance abuse and how chronic use strengthens these changes can increase motivation and desire to stop using.

In the criminal system, many incarcerated adults developed addictions during their adolescence. As a result, many people find themselves in the prison system due to a lack of necessary life skills, having developed instead a pervasive pattern of negative cognitive and behavioral interpersonal styles. This in turn interfered with their development of adequate cognitive and emotional skills to appropriately deal with everyday stressors. In addition to a self-defeating belief system, many incarcerated individuals have significant problems with impulse control and anger. Most of their problems can be traced back to the interference addiction had on the normal development of their adolescent brain as the frontal lobes had not fully developed such "executive" functions as decision making, judgment, and impulse control.

Problems with impulse control interfere with the development of other important cognitive and social skills that allow for more positive and successful social interactions and the acquisition and refinement of academic and occupational skills. Problems with impulse control increase the appeal of substances, which act quickly in the brain to numb perceptual experience. Over a relatively short period of time, this becomes the preferred method of "dealing with" emotional pain, and the behavior of substance abuse becomes a cyclic pattern as it leads to interpersonal chaos and increased emotional pain. Sadly, for many people in the prison system, the chronic use of alcohol and other intoxicating substances has led them down a path of self-destructive behaviors, which ultimately resulted in their loss of personal freedom.

Awareness Training

As discussed earlier, substances which activate dopamine receptors in the reward circuit of the brain can result in permanent changes after long-term usage. The adolescent brain is still developing, and substance use has a more damaging effect in a shorter period of time than for adult brains. This is due to neurological immaturity and the interference drug use has on developing systems in the brain, particularly the frontal lobes. On the more positive side, the adolescent brain, due to the gift of youth, is better able to "bounce back" to normal functioning than an older adult brain which is all the more reason to stop before too much time goes by and some or all damage becomes irreversible.

The age of initial use of alcohol and other substances appears to be getting younger each decade. Currently, the average age of first-time use of alcohol and marijuana is between ages twelve and seventeen, one year younger than the previous decade (National Survey on Drug Use and Health 2005). The long-term impact of this trend on our society is yet to be seen.

Emotional intelligence is a product of the interaction between the prefrontal cortex and the limbic system. It is different from intelligence as defined by academic success. It is defined by how well one is able to pick up on social cues and to successfully engage with others. Adolescents who, for a variety of reasons, are less sophisticated in picking up on social cues can be said to have impaired emotional intelligence. As we mature, our frontal lobes exercise more regulation over impulsive and reactive behavior, but for individuals with delays in this maturation process such as individuals with ADHD, emotional intelligence lags, and they are less well equipped to deal with emotionally charged situations in social settings. Over time, such individuals are more likely to abuse substances than their peers due to greater social phobia from their lack of social sophistication and will subsequently develop a reliance on substances to feel less anxious and to believe that they are "fitting in."

In addition to the shift from seeking natural sources of pleasure to substance-induced pleasure, deficits in mood regulation from repeated drug use present additional challenges in the earlier stages of recovery. Interference with brain development due to neural plasticity, resulting in increased numbers of less sensitive dopamine receptors and neural associations related to "incentive stimuli," further reduce the adolescent's capacity to respond effectively to everyday stress.

Emotional intelligence also has to do with an ability to regulate one's own moods. Increased mood instability and lowered tolerance for stress increases the adolescent's frequency and level of anxiety and depression as well as anger and sometimes, feelings of rage. Not having acquired ways to effectively self-calm, they resort to using, in an increasingly unsuccessful effort to "feel normal."

Difficulties with affect regulation maintain the addiction cycle. Adolescents suffering from co-occurring disorders are not able to sustain abstinence on their own for a long-enough period of time for their neurobiology to correct itself, and difficulties in affect regulation become a lifelong hindrance and a pattern of unstable moods. In addition to individual therapy that is directed at actively changing how one thinks, it is imperative that the adolescent (or anyone struggling with addiction) learn ways to become more self-aware. Developing the ability to self-calm is an essential skill, which in turn decreases the power of emotional triggers that can lead to relapse.

Emotional intelligence can be taught through cognitive therapy and methods such as meditation that teach how to self-calm. Relaxation training and meditation reduce the level of anxiety that may be experienced from perceived stressful social situations. Meditation is different from relaxation training, however, in that the point is not simply to learn how to relax but to improve the overall quality of thought, leading to better concentration and a calmer mind.

Meditation involves focusing inward, away from external distractions, to achieve greater calm and peace of mind. Hindu and Buddhist meditation are two ancient forms of meditation that have been used to improve concentration. The Buddhist method of meditation involves a focus on increasing awareness. Through this practice, one can develop a heightened ability to observe oneself and one's emotional reaction to events calmly, without getting trapped in them. Meditation increases awareness of the "now," and contrary to perception that it helps one to drift away on a pink cloud, meditation is thought to teach one how to be more aware.

Meditation at its simplest level involves the practice of breathing while in a relaxed position and pushing thoughts out of one's head. This method doesn't involve chanting, levitating, or anything but breathing. While focusing on breathing and pushing out ruminating and negative thoughts, one can enter into a calm and peaceful state of mind, without the potential chaos and stress of thinking. The purpose is to enter a zone of being fully absorbed in the moment and to experience life without thinking about it. It really is that simple.

Mindfulness is based on meditation and Eastern philosophy and involves a shift from other cognitive approaches. It doesn't stay focused on a specific thought but opens the focus to the experience and context in which the thought occurs, without holding a value or judgment on the thought. "Our monkey mind, as Buddhists call the internal chaos, keeps us swinging from past regrets to future worries, leaving little time for the here and now" (Kalb 2004). Thought is examined, moving away from the more chaotic and emotional mind to a more logic-based perspective. This approach is based on the theory that by changing how you experience your emotional reaction to your thoughts, you will be able to slowly change how you see things (Segal et al. 2002).

The adaptation of meditation into "mindfulness" meditation was started by Jon Kabat-Zinn in 1979. It was based on the Eastern practice of meditation and employed as a technique what he termed "mindfulness-based stress reduction." He used this form of meditation as a way to assist people in their ability to reduce stress and to tolerate intensive life challenges such as chronic pain and serious illness. According to Jon Kabat-Zinn, this technique improves quality of life and helps counter everyday stress and anxiety: "We are driven by the urgent, miss the important and then wind up a lot of the time being unhappy" (Kabat-Zinn 2010).

The purpose of engaging in mindfulness meditation is to achieve a quiet or calm awareness of oneself without negative emotions or judgmental thoughts. The field of psychology has adapted the concept of mindfulness as a cognitive therapeutic approach to treat people with chronic negative emotional states such as depression and self-destructive patterns of behavior. This awareness involves improving observation of one's emotional reaction to a particular event in a rational and nonemotional manner. Mindfulness combined with cognitive behavioral therapy improves an individual's awareness of their emotional reaction to negative and stressful experiences and reduces their feeling of being overwhelmed by their own emotions.

Both meditation and mindfulness training develop important mental skills that help an individual maintain sobriety by achieving greater peace of mind. Developing an ability to shift focus outside the potential distortion of emotions can be especially helpful in the early stages of sobriety when the fractured mind can generate a junkyard of emotional and self-defeating thoughts.

Whereas meditation is the art of focusing on the moment without thought, mindfulness involves focusing on the immediate experience and adopting an open and nonjudgmental awareness of thoughts and feelings one is experiencing in that moment. This technique involves an active effort to regulate one's ability to pay attention to the moment without succumbing to painful emotional feelings. In this self-calming mental skill, emotions are not ignored or controlled but accepted while learning how to move out of the painful, downward spiraling they can produce. Negative emotions are balanced with positive memories as well and are similar to cognitive therapy in the sense that the painful emotional states are decatastrophized. One learns to place powerful painful emotions into perspective by learning to not be drawn into an obsessive emotional loop.

Learning how to be "mindful" is especially valuable in achieving and maintaining sobriety. Not only is an adolescent in early recovery forced to deal with a barrage of emotions to which they have previously responded to by "numbing out," they may also need to reckon with the very real consequences of their drug use history such as a loss of family or peer support; educational, occupational, and legal setbacks; and diminished health. Many adolescents in early recovery have little experience dealing with any of these problems during their using days and are now also picking up the pieces of their fractured lives.

Part of an integrated treatment program provides alternatives to drug use. It is not possible for someone to "just say no" when they have no other way of dealing with emotional pain. Mindfulness training can provide one additional method of coping without falling into relapse. This method of self-calming provides a depth that can be lacking in a purely cognitive behavioral approach to treatment because not all problems in life are due to dysfunctional thoughts and may require a capacity to self-calm when things really are not going well. This practice teaches the individual how to accept and experience negative emotions without experiencing them as intense and overwhelming sensations. Painful experiences are not denied but rather are accepted without the intensity of painful emotional turmoil. Teaching cognitive skills with mindfulness training provides the adolescent with additional ways to establish and maintain recovery by reducing the triggers of intense negative emotions.

Social Support Systems

Earlier studies about addiction and recovery typically focused on alcoholism. They were based on substantially less scientific knowledge about how the brain works than is available with current research. The concept of the "disease model" was more about viewing alcoholism as a progressive disorder that resulted in health issues from long-term heavy drinking as well as the increasing difficulty in cessation of drinking over time, than as a medical disorder in itself. Alcoholism and other addictions were also held as the cause of mental illness such as depression and not medical disorders in themselves. The disease model was used only figuratively to reduce negative self-perception and to encourage abstinence. Relapse however, according to this ideology, was due to a lack of conviction and integrity and viewed as a weakness of character rather than due to having a real disease that required medical attention.

Many 12-step models move the power from the individual to something over which they have no power to control, hence, the concept of giving up control to a "higher power." This is generally more helpful if the individual already has a firm religious conviction in a higher power. Although 12-step programs work for many, they do not work for everyone, and almost half of the people who enter such a program relapse. This is not to demean 12-step programs in any way as compared to other unilateral methods of treatment (vs. integrated treatment). Twelve-step programs have relatively high success rates (fifty-two percent) compared to other single focused recovery methods and can make all the difference in personal recovery. When 12-step programs are combined with other forms of treatment, however, the likelihood for sustained sobriety is increased and should therefore be considered as part of an integrated treatment approach.

One of the clinical concerns to referring an individual to 12-step programs is the potential sabotage of other types of treatment. Some people in 12-step programs have mistaken some basic concepts in the doctrine, take issue with psychology and psychiatry, and disparage the use of psychiatric medication. Some people also misunderstand the concept of "a higher power" as pertaining only to their particular religious convictions and believe that their personal religious belief has identified the only true "higher power." Contrary to this, the ideology of "higher power" is more based on how the individual chooses to see their higher power or God. No one has the ultimate answer for another. Care should be taken, therefore, in choosing a support group that is best suited for oneself on an individual basis. If you don't feel comfortable in a particular group, don't give up on the concept of 12-step programs; try other groups until you find a better fit with your philosophical or religious belief system.

Other models of treatment of alcoholism were centered on personal responsibility and willpower. The focus of treatment was primarily on behavior (i.e., to reduce drinking). Until fairly recently, other factors involved in addiction were not yet understood. Talk therapy (psychotherapy) alone has not been found to be effective in establishing sobriety and only marginally effective in maintaining sobriety (Seligman 1993). The use of medications was introduced as adjuncts to treatment or to reduce the symptoms of withdrawal. Still, the focus was not yet on treating the underlying psychological issues that can lead to addiction.

One earlier medication treatment that focused only on behavior was aversion therapy. Aversion therapy involves the use of Antabuse, which is a medication that causes severe nausea and shortness of breath if alcohol is consumed. This was not a very effective method as the patients would frequently simply stop taking their medication to resume drinking. In this treatment, the focus was only on the actual behavior of drinking alcohol and power was put outside the individual.

Another earlier concept that again focused on behavior referred to people who suffered from addiction as having an "addictive" personality. This referred to deficits of willpower and character and was not referring to neurological differences due to a genetic and biologically based etiology. People believed that environment and upbringing were primarily responsible for the development of addiction. An important study that debunked this belief was done in by George Vaillant in 1995 and focused on men who suffered from alcoholism.

George Vaillant's study demonstrated that contrary to popular belief, positive factors such as a happy and relatively normal childhood environment, high education, high intelligence, and good "mothering" did not reduce the risk of alcoholism. This study did find that the absence of a social support system was a strong predictor of an unsuccessful recovery from alcoholism (Vaillant 1995). Social supports such as family, marriage, positive friends, and children were identified as important in establishing and maintaining sobriety. In this study, other community-based support systems such as strong religious ties in one's faith and 12-step programs were also found to be powerful sources of support for maintaining sobriety.

Group Therapy

"People need people—for initial and continued survival, for socialization, for the pursuit of satisfaction. No one—not the dying, not the outcast, not the mighty—transcends the need for human contact" (Yalom 1995, 21). One of the largest hidden obstacles to recovery is the painful depth of loneliness that can occur as one gives up old "friends" (who were really just substance-using associates). In early sobriety, the adolescent is in a transitory stage during which time he or she may still be shunned by many or all non-drug-using acquaintances and family members whom he or she may have harmed, offended or frightened in some way. On top of social isolation, during early stages of sobriety, the brain must adjust not only to detoxification and operating without substances but without normal levels of neurotransmitters that reduce pain and cause the sensation of pleasure. This is why it is essential that early recovery includes a supportive environment of family and supportive group membership, whether in-house or community based.

Peer-support group therapy is therefore an important component of an integrated treatment process. This therapy modality provides validation, feedback, and emotional support during what can be an inordinately painful, frustrating, and lonely period of time. In addition to in-house peer support, individuals need to be encouraged to seek out community support such as church or school-based youth groups and 12-step programs.

In later sobriety, peer support can also be part of aftercare as part of a continuation of treatment. After active involvement in treatment, the adolescent or young adult continues to meet with peers through an alumni support group that provides mutual support and guidance. This will reduce feelings of isolation and aid in the process of transitioning into new social environments without falling back to old drug-using peers out of loneliness and feelings of isolation.

Family Therapy

Family therapy is another valuable way to support the adolescent in their treatment, especially during early sobriety. One model of family group therapy involves having multiple adolescents and their families interact in a group format. This system can facilitate treatment by providing additional support, validation, modeling, and encouraging better conflict-resolution skills of family members. One of the treatment goals in family group therapy are to remove the focus of the adolescent as the "identified patient," to better understand how to reduce tension and triggers in the home while allowing family members to express how the adolescent's drug use impacts them.

The primary goal of family therapy in treating addiction, however, is to help support the adolescent maintain sobriety by reducing conflict and stress in the family environment. For optimal treatment to be achieved, confidence and trust must be established. On this point, the family therapist should ideally be a different therapist from the primary therapist to avoid perceived betrayal of the therapist (siding with the parent) or splitting (perceived as siding with the parents or the adolescent), both of which can contaminate the therapeutic bond.

Creating Structure

A lack of structure of daily activities, as well as forgotten hobbies and non-substance-related interests, also significantly contribute to relapse. A very bright young man once explained a major part of his difficulty in remaining sober was that "getting high is something I do with my friends, in between doing other things."

During early recovery, time management or tracking how you spend your time can help in structuring time. Journaling and writing down how time is spent can be a way to identify time during the day that needs to be filled to avoid boredom and loneliness, both of which can lead to relapse. If your day is planned out ahead of time, it is also less likely that you will spend time dwelling on negative events and feelings. It is better at this point to be busy and to distract from negative thoughts and memories.

There are two fundamental facts well understood by psychologists: The first fact is that every behavior has a function. The second fact is that you cannot eliminate a behavior unless you replace it with another behavior that serves the same function. Therefore, another component to an integrated system of recovery is helping the newly recovering individual reconnect with old interests or establish new interests to replace the behavior that they have been employing to serve a particular function or purpose.

What exactly does this mean? For example, perhaps smoking is a method you use to calm down when you are very angry, but you are trying to stop smoking. You must learn to replace smoking behavior with a more positive behavior that achieves the same purpose. It must be antithetical or directly opposite to the behavior you are attempting to avoid. In this instance, you might choose weight lifting or running as they both require a lot of mental focus and physical energy and serve to redirect your body and mind's energy from the anger you feel.

Another method might be to implement some skills that help you relax and draw you away from your angry thoughts. Of course, it all depends on the urgency of your need to calm down. In the moment, it is better to draw upon meditation and mindfulness skills you will learn to calm down quickly; later, you can have a good workout to kick up your endorphins as well. Consider this: when you have developed a physical regime and are seeing the physical results of improved muscle mass, skin tone, and overall health, you will be more resistant to throw these achievements away by using when faced with a trigger.

Purpose underlies activities such as going back to school or gaining employment. The long-term plan of establishing independence and the ability to achieve satisfying work is the purpose for going back and completing school. To achieve this outcome, it is necessary not only to work on recovery but also to commit to getting up every day and attending school or training. While this may be difficult initially, it will become easier as time goes by, especially while achieving milestones along the way.

Family, peer, and other support is essential to overcome feelings of hopelessness or reminders of past failures that may arise along the path to recovery and occupational success. The only way to truly achieve a sense of self-respect is by doing and achieving. Achieving will naturally follow a commitment to doing. You go to school and you get your diploma. You go to work and you get a paycheck. The more success you achieve, the more you will believe in your ability to be successful—pretty simple when you think it through.

Equally important, and perhaps more so during your early phase of recovery, is developing new behaviors that can be enjoyable and rewarding as well as filling up free time. Good examples of behaviors that help with sobriety are those that stir up your body's natural endorphins. Weight lifting, running, bicycling, dancing, swimming, or any cardiovascular workout washes the body with natural endorphins. The good feelings associated with this natural release of feel-good chemicals are longer lasting than artificial intoxicants and do not have the negative effects of withdrawal when they dissipate from your body. There is no comedown, no pain, but rather a decrease in negative emotions such as anger or depression.

Whereas physical activities help your mind and body, art, poetry, music, and writing can allow you to express your emotions and to develop a deeper connection and understanding of yourself. We are all inclined to express ourselves differently and have preferences for different sensory experiences such as auditory, visual, taste, touch, or movement. If you do not already have an idea of which artistic expression best suits you, try them all. Money limitations are important, but not every activity has to be expensive. Writing and drawing only require a pencil or pen and paper and can be the easiest to implement. Getting an inexpensive set of children's watercolors, pencils, crayons, and even colored chalk can result in a rewarding sense of visual expression. You never know until you try.

Over time, your brain will reprogram, and the experienced level of pleasant feelings from these activities will increase. If this seems unlikely, consider this example of how our brain can be corrupted and then reprogrammed: Take a piece of candy versus an apple. If you never ate candy, you would naturally enjoy the apple. Although you may prefer the candy at this point in your life, having corrupted your sense of taste by eating candy, over time, you will lose your cravings for candy and learn once again, to enjoy the apple. It just takes time.

Our ancestors have evolved with a preference for sweet foods due to the need for calories and a lack of availability of food. Sweet foods have more calories and therefore were valuable during times when people couldn't run to the store to get food. Candy has a more concentrated level of sweetness and calories than an apple; therefore, our taste and brain will prefer the candy. Over time, if you eat enough candy, you will lose a taste for fruits and prefer the candy. If you give up the candy, you will crave it for some time, and the apple will not taste as good initially. The longer you stay away from the candy, however, the better the apple will start to taste. In fact, if you stay away from candy long enough and you eat it sometime later, it will probably taste too sweet.

Same thing with salty foods—feel free to experiment to prove this to yourself. Avoid extra salt and salty foods for several months. Then, have a cup of some salty noodle soup and see how it really tastes. I guarantee you will not be able to eat and enjoy the whole thing.

Our sense of taste can become corrupted when given a diet of salty or sugary food versus more natural and wholesome food. Our brains produce chemicals such as dopamine and serotonin that make us feel good. Alcohol and other illicit substances bombard the same areas of the brain with a concentrated dose of dopamine and interfere with our natural production and absorption of these chemicals. The high you get from running or working out may or may not be as intense as what you may momentarily experience from certain substances, but the good feelings last longer and are good for you! You just need to be patient and give it time. The longer you can stay clean, the easier it is to remain clean. A friend once told me how she views her sobriety: "Every day clean and sober, I purify and heal myself . . . Every day clean and sober, I am reborn."

PART FIVE

The Bridge

Public Policy

Many institutions such as the Substance Abuse and Mental Health Services Administration, National Institute of Mental Health, National Institute on Drug Abuse, and the National Institute on Alcohol Abuse and Alcoholism have been instrumental in research that helps assess and recommend methods to improve integration of various multileveled governmental entities and mental health providers for the prevention and treatment of substance abuse disorders. Unfortunately, findings in this research concluded that although treatment is theoretically available, it is not readily accessed. Further, it has been found that there is a deficit in "the will, social policies, and collaborative strategies to adequately support the healthy development of the nation's young people" (O'Connell et al. 2009).

Overall, research has identified a need for more funding and coordination among state agencies to increase access to treatment.

> Officials at the local, state, and federal levels all play a role in mental health promotion and the prevention of MEB[3] disorders. Many providers and agencies are responsible for the care, protection, or support of young people: the child welfare, education, and juvenile justice systems, as well as medical and mental health care providers and community organizations. Yet resources within these agencies are

---

[3] mental, emotional, and behavioral disorders

scattered, not coordinated, and often do not effectively
support prevention programs or policies. (National Academy
of Sciences 2009)

Research has also identified a need for increased public education
to improve awareness of mental health and substance abuse and
to reduce the stigma of mental health and addiction or substance
abuse disorders. By stigmatizing and negatively labeling individuals
with co-occurring disorders, our society has been minimizing and
unfortunately prolonging a very real plight. Adolescents with mental
illness and substance abuse disorders are more likely to be cast out
from society than to receive help. No one wants to believe it can
happen to their own children, but substance abuse disorders cross all
socioeconomic barriers. Our society must come to terms with ending
the social delusion that anyone is shielded from this modern-day
plague.

Although much of the focus of research has been on prevention,
concepts can be pulled from it to improve identification and treatment
of adolescents with co-occurring disorders (O'Connell et al. 2009).
Involvement of members of the community—including parents,
educators, child welfare, health care providers, and the criminal justice
system—in the identification of both mental health and substance
abuse disorders begins with increased awareness and an understanding
of indicators of adolescent mental health and substance abuse
disorders. Greater awareness will result in the identification of at-risk
teens and generate referrals to the care they need. It will not only
benefit individuals and their families but will also ultimately benefit
our society as it will reduce crime, human tragedy and governmental
expenditures in housing incarcerated individuals, and shift funding
toward more proactive and positive social causes.

Law and Access to Care

Access to care may be further impeded by an overzealous concern for liability by health care providers. Requiring parental consent to reduce potential liability may drive too many adolescents away from treatment. Requiring parental consent is not necessarily in the best interest of all young people. For various reasons, not every teenager has parents who are willing, concerned enough, or able to give consent to treatment.

Mental health and drug abuse treatment in many states does not require parental consent if certain conditions are met. The conditions relevant for mental health and drug abuse treatment include the adolescent being twelve years of age or older, mature enough to understand what occurs in treatment, and able to comprehend and actively participate in treatment. Under the California Family Code, the minor would also have to be documented as to "present a danger of serious physical or mental harm to self or others without the mental health treatment" (National Center for Youth Law, 2003 and 2007, Cal. Family Code §6924). Additionally, "a minor who is 12 years of age or older may consent to medical care and counseling relating to the diagnosis and treatment of a drug or alcohol-related problem" (Cal. Family Code § 6929b).

Despite this conditional authority to provide treatment to adolescents, many providers still require parental consent before treatment can begin. This is primarily due to concerns about liability if a parental objection was ever raised as the provider would have to demonstrate that the minor did meet the necessary conditions. "The health care provider is required to involve a parent or guardian unless the health care provider decides that involvement is inappropriate. This decision must be documented in the minor's record" (National Center for Youth Law 2003, California Family Code § 6924).

Involvement of the adolescent's family, however, no matter how dysfunctional they may be, might provide emotional support at some level. It is usually a good idea to try to improve family dynamics, as the adolescent will only benefit from whatever support they can get. Adolescence is also a time during which many teens and their parents are at odds and this possibility should be taken into account. Family therapy may also help resolve some behaviors by family members that contribute to the adolescent's psychological issues. If the choice must include involvement of a dysfunctional family or the adolescent cannot participate in treatment, however, the choice is simple as it will be better than no treatment at all.

Inversely, consent for treatment does not require the minor to give consent (National Center for Youth Law 2007, California Family Code § 6929f). An unwillingness of the adolescent to participate in treatment can sabotage treatment, and it is preferable to find a way to engage them at some level to hopefully develop trust and some degree of motivation. Regardless of their initial motivation to receive help, however, it is still better to get an adolescent started at some level of treatment rather than to have them left on their own.

Compromise is always a good thing. Studies have indicated that the outcome of drug treatment is less successful when the adolescent is required, against their objection, to obtain parental consent by the treatment provider. There is solution to this potential roadblock, which is a "passive" parental consent to treatment rather than "active" parental consent (Smith et al. 2009). Passive consent involves obtaining written parental consent for treatment but with the understanding and agreement by the parent(s) to respect their child's privacy. This means that with certain safety-related exceptions, parents are not generally privy to information provided by the adolescent to the provider while in treatment. This may prove to be essential as it may promote a greater degree of trust and willingness to be more forthcoming by the adolescent about his or her substance abuse to the provider.

Without treatment, addiction can ultimately develop to a level that will result in disability, death or incarceration due to behaviors that are directly (e.g., possession or under the influence) and indirectly (e.g., burglary, robbery, reckless, or assaultive behavior) related to drug abuse. People representative of all age groups, genders, sexual orientations, races or ethnicities, cultures, spiritual or religious belief systems, and socioeconomic backgrounds are incarcerated for crimes that are, more often than not, rooted to their addiction.

During a juvenile court proceeding, a judge stated to the young person standing in front of him, "If you are unable to stay clean, we have a rehabilitation program for you." Despite this claim, the criminal justice system generally doesn't provide an effective mental health or rehabilitation program for youth or adults. Once an individual is placed into the prison system, it is unfortunately late in the game, there is often no real treatment, and there is a greater focus by that individual on "getting over and getting by" (i.e., surviving). Individuals who really need and want help are often held back by fear of being singled out as "crazy" or "weak" by other inmates and, therefore, typically try to hide their symptoms. In addition, jails and prisons, despite all best efforts, are far from drug-free environments.

Ironically, despite its limitations, the prison and jail system are too often the only access to any semblance of treatment incarcerated individuals with co-occurring disorders ever experience. Many such individuals have claimed that the "good thing about being locked up" was that it was the only time in their life that they were able to get any mental health treatment. Surely, there must be a better way to help our youth.

A Perfect World

Earlier, the "no wrong door" policy was discussed. This system would allow access to an appropriate provider of addiction treatment or mental health treatment, regardless of which care provider was the point of first contact. The system as stated, however, really only addresses the coordination between different agencies or providers of communicating with one another and referring individuals to the treatment they themselves do not provide. A drug counselor would refer an individual with psychological concerns to a psychologist or psychiatrist and vice versa. In contrast, fully integrated system of care providers would directly provide treatment for individuals suffering from addiction and mental illness.

Even if there was an abundance (which there is not) of integrated treatment providers, there would still be the obstacle of how to access that care. Adolescents with co-occurring disorders are not typically referred or granted access to needed treatment. They are more likely seen as "troubled" and are punished for their behavior. They typically end up being dismissed to "continuing schools," which only serve to increase their sense of failure and access to other adolescents who have greater access to drugs, dropping out of school, being kicked out of their homes, and eventually becoming hopeless and homeless "drug addicts" until they either die or are arrested for a crime related to their drug addiction.

Referrals to drug treatment may also be hampered by a lack of awareness that the adolescent is abusing drugs. Parents and educators, who may have no experience with using drugs themselves, can be oblivious to symptoms of drug use. Unfortunately, the legal system tends to focus on addiction as a problem to be dealt with criminally, overlooking underlying or comorbid mental health factors. Failed but still funded drug prevention programs of this mind-set focus on attempting to teach youth to "just say no," with no understanding or focus on mental health factors that contribute to addiction. There is also a void of information available for most families of how and where to get the help they need for at-risk youth. Due to our educational, health care, and legal system methods of dealing with the problem of drug addiction and mental illness, there are many lost opportunities for an adolescent to get identified as at risk and to gain access to the treatment they need.

Families and educators need to be taught how to recognize symptoms of mental illness and drug use. Once an adolescent is identified as having a problem with drugs and alcohol, the more typical response of the educational system is to exclude them from regular or any school. Our educational system needs a better method of identifying and referring at-risk adolescents to treatment. Additionally, primary care and other medical providers can do a better job in the identification and appropriate referral of adolescents who are struggling with mental illness and/or addiction. Many adolescents are seen by their primary care provider for physical symptoms that may be indicative of an underlying addiction or mental health disorders. Dentists also treat adolescents and are knowledgeable about dental indicators of substance abuse and can also be a source of feedback for parents to help teens get the help they may need.

Despite the potential sources of identification and referral of youth with co-occurring disorders to treatment, parents are all too often left to struggle on their own in getting help for their children. Even if parents are able to find treatment programs to help their child, the cost can be prohibitive. Addiction and mental health disorders that impact our youth are simply not treated on par with medical disorders, a practice which is simply unacceptable.

The criminal justice system currently channels identified youth into juvenile systems, which, at best, provides narrowly focused and ineffective treatment for addiction or mental illness. Too many youthful "offenders" are really suffering from co-occurring disorders and end up becoming institutionalized without ever getting the treatment they need. If a referral system was in place for first offenders of drug use that provided access to a true integrated treatment program rather than an introduction into the criminal system or to a criminal justice-based "drug" program, our society would not only save money but also, more importantly, reduce the current rate of unacceptable loss of human potential.

At-risk youth will typically begin having an academic downturn and behavioral problems in school before their problems become severe enough to get the attention of law enforcement. One way to expedite consensual awareness in the earlier stages of substance abuse is by the promotion of an open and nondefensive communication between adolescents and their parents, caretakers, and school. Ideally, this could involve an understanding with local law enforcement to not criminally identify or label "at-risk" youth. Rather, this system would entail a nonpunitive approach that facilitates access to treatment rather than punishment for at-risk youth. Additionally, parents or caretakers should be encouraged to attend substance abuse education classes to increase their awareness of the drug culture, addiction, and mental illness.

Unfortunately, schools too often approach what they perceive as behavioral problems by getting rid of "problem" students through expulsion or transfer to a nontraditional "independent studies" or other form of quasi-education program. This may appear to solve the problem but in reality throws younger and less experienced teens together with older teens that likely have greater access to a wider variety of illicit substances.

The proposed "perfect world" system would involve interaction between different agencies such as education and treatment providers with an agreement that honesty on the part of the adolescent will not result in any negative educational or legal consequences. This system calls for a nonpunitive and care-oriented response to identified "at-risk" youth. In this proposed system, for example, if a teacher was concerned about a student, he or she would make a phone call to the parents and a referral to the school psychologist or counselor rather than a referral to campus security. Ultimately, this should result in providing referrals to a treatment provider. All referrals should be confidential and not included in the student's general educational records. An overall atmosphere of support and collaboration would exist between parents, educators, and students with the goal of providing help rather than punishment.

PART SIX

Evolution

Recovery Philosophy

What is the overall philosophy and goal of an integrated system of treatment and care? The primary goal of course is for reaching out and helping our youth who are suffering from addiction and symptoms of mental health disorders. There is a crisis in this country that spreads across urban cities, suburbia, and the rural countryside. This crisis is the unacceptable loss of so many young people to the ultimate outcome of substance abuse: death or incarceration. The primary recovery philosophy is to pull our youth out of their downward spiral and to get them on track to where they need to be rather than where they will be if they do not get help.

Suicide is the third leading cause of death among teens and young adults. A 2009 study conducted by the County of Orange Health Care Agency found that during that year, close to 2,700 people intentionally inflicted self-harm and over 260 completed suicide. Significantly, the study identified that the major risk factors of these self-inflicted injuries and suicides are mental illness and substance abuse. The study also found that in that same year, the majority of people treated in the emergency department also suffered from mental illness and substance abuse (Orange County Health Care Agency 2009).

Incarcerated youth and adults represent the other side of this dismal rainbow. I have met many young adults who believe that being incarcerated saved their life. They reported that the level of their drug use was so high prior to their arrest that they believed that but for having been arrested, they would have died of overdose, dehydration, malnutrition, or physical exhaustion. What a tragic way for someone to get help, if they really get help at all. We need to reach our youth before they end up going down this path, because incarceration is not the solution, nor does it likely result in rehabilitation.

Rehabilitation in the penal system doesn't generally have a positive outcome for the average nonviolent, non-gang-affiliated inmate and much less so for people who suffer from co-occurring disorders. Largely due to increasing budgetary restraints over the past decade, the substance abuse prevention programs, education, and vocational training programs in prison have taken the biggest cuts and are mostly nonexistent.

Currently, mental health programs, which historically have taken a backseat to medical treatment, have also been slashed. To save money, psychologists who were placed into the prison system, due to lawsuits from maltreatment of mentally ill inmates, are now being replaced through attrition with staff without the same level of clinical skills or training. Substance abuse programs have also been slashed to bare bones, and each counselor must simultaneously treat groups of inmates so large that most people in the group cannot hear what is being said by the counselor.

The only possible "benefit" to incarceration is no longer due to rehabilitation but due to the real punishment of losing one's freedom and time, which, in itself, may be a deterrent to future drug use. However, although considerably more expensive to obtain, drugs are widely prevalent in prison. Further, the elements in prison only foster increased criminal thinking and behavior. Young men refer to the juvenile detention centers as "gladiator school," meaning if you do survive, you do so by developing violent and deceptive antisocial skills.

The purpose for reviewing how the current system really works is simply a reality check. It is hard to look at your child or yourself and see how badly things can work out, but this is something that needs to be honestly addressed. When our loved ones are caught up in the cycle of addiction, it is very hard to see past the moment, but it has to be done. Drug abuse is a crisis situation and not something that someone can pull out of without help. Too many people feel that if only the individual would toughen up, they could recover, but this is misguided. It needs to be clear that once addiction is in place, there is no way out on one's own. The Jim Morrison biography, which addressed his heroin addiction, *No One Here Gets Out Alive* (Hopkins and Sugerman, 1980), was and is the reality of addiction.

We must help adolescents pull out of their downward spiral into the rabbit hole. To achieve sustained recovery, they need to understand how addiction works and the real damage chronic addiction causes as well as to replace hopelessness with hope. Group and family support in addition to individual therapy will also help them feel supported and better able to achieve and maintain sobriety. In addition to achieving stability and sobriety, they will develop a capacity for better insight and improved judgment and learn how to set and work toward goals. Ultimately, treatment will set them on the path toward improved personal dignity and self-esteem.

Coordination of Care

In addition to facilitating more successful interactions between the adolescent and his or her community, active communication with providers of medical treatment is vital to a successful outcome of treatment. Coordination of care means active involvement between the therapist, drug counselor, case manager, psychiatrist, and any other care providers. Open communication between providers will better ensure treatment and medication compliance and tracking of symptom reduction or a reemergence of symptoms (relapse).

In addition to treating psychiatric symptoms, medications can help reduce pain associated with withdrawal and improve sobriety. Certain medications block opioid receptors to reduce euphoria from drug use and pain from withdrawal, which also helps the individual maintain sobriety. There is a dramatic improvement in sustained sobriety from opioids in particular when there is a combination of therapy and medical treatment using agonist and antagonist medications (Miller and Rollnick 2009). Other medications have been demonstrated to help reduce cravings for other substances such as alcohol and nicotine.

It is hard for adolescents in the early stage of sobriety to adhere to medical recommendations for several reasons, one being that psychopharmacological medications do not work as instantaneously as illicit substances. This is one of the primary causes for noncompliance to medication recommendations, as well as lack of family or peer support and unidentified true motivation to change. Active encouragement and support by the therapist, family, peer support, and community support systems during early stages of treatment improve compliance with treatment through external controls. This is crucial as there are not likely to be many intrinsic internal rewards in the very beginning of sobriety.

Some treatment programs utilize monetary or other tangible rewards (called contingency management) to reinforce maintained sobriety. Addiction involves overactivation of the reward circuit, and over time, due to neuroplasticity, there is a decrease in the normal function of this circuit, thus making the individual less responsive to things that used to provide pleasure (Koob and Le Moa 2005). Contingency management may make up for this loss by supplying an extrinsic reward such as tokens, certificates, trinkets, or money until the intrinsic reward system (the reward circuit or pleasure center) begins to function more normally.

PART SEVEN

Personal Genesis

Looking Forward

The terms "addiction" and "mental illness" hold powerful, negative social connotations. Adolescents who suffer from both disorders typically end up marginalized and shunned by society. Often, due to their erratic and increasingly drug-related criminal behaviors over time, they are cut off from their own families. Suffering from co-occurring disorders does not typically result in a good outcome. The prognosis for an adolescent who suffers from addiction and mental illness is poor, and the rate of adolescents who do recover and live a full life has been far from acceptable. The research and knowledge is there, yet there continues to be a disconnection between research-based advances in understanding addiction and mental illness and available treatment for adolescents who are struggling with their illnesses.

Depression results from a combination of multiple factors. Unless recognized and treated, it traps one's spirit into a psychologically dark and hopeless place. When a depressed adolescent discovers that a particular substance relieves him of his emotional pain, no matter how short and costly the reprieve, he will come back again and again for it. The adolescent brain is still developing, and this process is arrested in varying degrees by addiction. Untreated psychological disorders such as bipolar disorder, major depressive disorder, and psychosis are medical disorders and, if left untreated over time, can result in an increase of symptoms, which can result in further neurological and psychological damage. The good news is that with treatment and time, due to the neuroplasticity of the brain, healing and a return to previous functioning is possible.

"Mental illness" is a term that is simply overinclusive and carries a negative connotation. This is unfortunate because due to the stigma attached to this term, adolescents, like many adults, do not like to be defined as having such. This results in a minimization or denial of symptoms to themselves and to others. As a result, adolescents are not likely to seek help and are more likely to escape emotional pain through behaviors that are self-destructive, such as self-mutilation, street racing, and unprotected sex with multiple partners or drug abuse. Additionally, symptoms of mental illness can be masked, mistaken, or written off as indications of drug use. Self-report of symptoms does not generally provide a full or accurate assessment when working with adult populations, and sensitivity to this is even more fundamentally important when working with the adolescent population.

Adolescents who suffer from co-occurring disorders typically abhor the label of mental illness and would rather focus on and even exaggerate their drug use to avoid discussing the depth of the emotional pain they feel. What is needed is a paradigm shift; rather than focus on the individual as having a mental illness, it would be more useful to define what his or her actual symptoms are and address the symptoms directly, without negative and stereotypical labels. Diagnostic labels are, after all, really only tools to help a clinician decide on a course of treatment or to bill insurance companies and do not, in any way, define a person. Perhaps simply the term "emotional pain" more accurately describes what an addicted and depressed adolescent suffers from than any diagnostic label.

An integrated system of care simply means treatment that addresses the person, not a label. Treatment should begin with establishing trust and needs to be flexible and adaptive to the individual's particular needs. Drug education and relapse prevention help the adolescent and his or her family develop a better understanding of how addiction and triggers work. Learning new perspectives and skills from mindfulness training and cognitive, group, and individual therapy as well as developing a personal motivation and internal system of control or accountability are all components of recovery. Family and community support and addressing real needs such as housing, education, money, and medical care are also integral parts of this system.

Our children are the future; they are a precious resource that we cannot continue to allow to be lost. Too many young people, intentionally and unintentionally, each and every day, die as a result of substance abuse. Recovery is possible, but it is not a simple and short-term process. The statistics for sustained recovery in the adolescent population indicate that most available treatments have not been effective. The brain takes years to fully recover and thirty to ninety days of treatment just does not work.

There has been an apparent disconnection between the research community and the clinical community. Research has identified evidence-based treatment protocols that are effective and promote sustained recovery, yet these programs do not seem to be readily available, and are certainly not affordable, for low- and middle-income families. Evidence-based research is what this proposed treatment program is based on, with the intention to not only remain evidence based but to also be a fluid model that constantly evolves to incorporate new information about conquering addiction.

A Time to Redefine

Our community needs a dramatic increase in evidence-based treatment centers to combat the rising increase of substance abuse of our youth. Adolescents and their families can expect to attain recovery. None need to do it alone, and certainly no one needs to give up hope. If you are reading this for yourself, you have taken the first step toward recovery. The next step is in shedding negative, self-perpetuating prophecies. You must redefine yourself as a pioneer or a maverick, shedding old concepts, labels, stereotypes, and anything that glues you to a cycle of negativity.

What is the definition of a maverick? A maverick is one who refuses to accept the status quo and who is willing to stand out from the crowd when necessary and redefine the world and himself or herself on their own terms. A maverick rejects that which he or she knows to be untrue and is willing to act in accordance to that belief. Mavericks are people who have been responsible for positive change throughout time. They are those brave individuals who have stepped out of their comfort zone by standing up and rejecting the status quo when they knew it was wrong—rejecting racism, sexism, elitism, and other rigid manners of thinking—and have been the force that has moved our world forward in a positive direction.

A society based on ignorance stigmatizes that which it doesn't understand. Despite how hard society may press, however, it cannot create a false reality by the promotion of negative stereotypes. The stereotype at issue is that "addicts" are somehow "bad" people, "weak" people, people who come from bad homes, people who are somehow lesser than others. Dismissing a huge segment of our population who suffer from co-occurring disorders as a problem that can be ignored is simply an attempt to shut out and stifle a reality that feels uncomfortable. This is also known as "magical thinking" and in this regard is a false sense of security that the problem of addiction cannot happen to oneself or members of one's family.

Anyone who is struggling with some form of addiction—whether cigarettes, alcohol, cocaine, methamphetamines, heroin, ecstasy, prescription pills, even food—can redefine himself or herself without the labels others have previously applied. Negative labels such as "addict" reduce an individual to a static, stereotyped object, erasing all that makes that person unique and important.

Imagine you are a very young and innocent child. Take it further and imagine you have newly arrived here from another planet, as did the fictional character Valentine in *Stranger in a Strange Land* (Heinlein 1961). Valentine had been the lone survivor of an earlier expedition of scientists to the planet Mars and had spent his youth on Mars, away from the daily complexity of human interactions on Earth. Although Valentine was already an adult in his twenties, he was challenged with what it was like to be a human on Earth. He was innocent, trusting, and lacked any critical interpretation of others and their behaviors. His manner of attempting to engage with others to fully understand their personal reality was defined by him as "to grok" (Heinlein 1961). In this fictional world, "grokking" was a Martian concept, which meant to attempt a pure and uncritical understanding of another at a depth so intimate and complete as to fully merge with the other person's sense and understanding of reality.

Now turn this concept onto yourself. Look at yourself from a fresh and accepting perspective; let go of the labels others have pasted on you. Forget any critical, negative, or hopeless manner in which you may view yourself and your past actions. Sit comfortably and close your eyes. At this moment, be nothing more than your immediate experience of smell, sound, and light. Experience these sensations without judgment or emotion, just notice them. Meditate on your core, your essence, the nature of what most defines you at this moment. Learn how to see or to "grok" yourself in this manner without bias or judgment, without looking back and judging.

You are not an "addict"; you struggle with addiction. You are not "bipolar" or "crazy"; you may have psychological and emotional difficulties. You may struggle with extreme and unpredictable mood states, but this does not define you! People who have psychological issues such as bipolar disorder or recurring depression are no different from people who struggle with other medical problems.

Diabetes, for example, is a medical disorder that can, among many complications, be accompanied by fluctuations in mood due to variations of blood sugar levels. If you have diabetes and your doctor told you to control your diet and take a particular medication, a reasonable individual who wanted to get better would comply. Both of these situations (bipolar disorder and diabetes) require some sort of intervention—it is that simple. There is no difference in that regard between what types of disorder you may be challenged with, only the name of the disorder and the treatment for that disorder. You cannot, however, expect everyone else to accept this simple truth; you can only control how you see things and what you do with the knowledge you are given.

There are different challenges people struggle with. Some people may struggle with medical illness, physical challenges, perceptual distortions, mood swings, depressed moods, anxiety, addiction, or any number of disorders or conditions. Any number of things can be a challenge, but that does not mean it is the end game. Problems you may be faced with are like branches on a tree, with you as the tree. Each branch is part of the tree, as are the leaves, flowers, trunk, and roots. Yet no one branch defines the tree, as the tree is more than any of its parts. The essence of the tree exists on its own merits; no one branch can solely define it. Therefore, no one branch that is ailing is enough cause for the tree to stop flourishing, as long as the branch is taken care of and the tree heals. With the right care, the tree can thrive.

You need to redefine yourself in a more positive yet realistic manner. The concept of "to grok" may sound strange, but it describes a hopeful effort to become more fully aware, to comprehend or relate to something without labels or preconceptions; and in this case, that happens to be you. The goal is to understand yourself without the usual self-critical thinking that has too often shut you down and left you discouraged. This is a crucial step in your recovery process—to fully accept yourself as a complete and unique person who may struggle with an addictive and psychological disorder but who is in no way defined by either.

Happiness

Recently, there was a short news report about happiness. During this segment, an unnamed wise and elderly woman provided her thoughts on happiness. In response to the question of how she has been able to stay happy throughout the years, she replied, "I focus on the good, think about the good, and don't worry about the bad." This golden philosophy suggests that many positive concepts of how to approach life may already be embedded within our culture.

One of those concepts is mindfulness, which is simply awareness of the actual moment you are experiencing. Although this concept was derived from the method of being aware and fully awake as taught in Zen Buddhism meditation, many people in Western culture are aware of and already refer to a similar mind state as "being in the zone," a state of absolute focus on what you are doing that typically occurs during intensive physical or creative moments. Another way to understand this state of "being in the moment" can be reflected in the common expression "Stopping to smell the roses."

Another different, but positive idea is the expression "Seize the moment." A concept most likely derived from ancient origins: "carpe diem," a phrase from a Latin poem by Horace, meaning "to seize the day" or from Hebrew "and if not now, when?"—all having the same meaning of acting on something now rather than putting it off. Similarly, mindfulness is a concept that has been widely understood but too often out of practice and forgotten. Mindfulness is simply living in the moment, savoring and enjoying the good, accepting but not being consumed by the bad.

Everyone has their demons. Some are more intense, more self-destructive and harder to overcome than others, and some can throw even the best of us down the rabbit hole. What is important to remember is that every time you fall, pick yourself up, and climb out of the rabbit hole of addiction, you get stronger and closer to your recovery. It can also be said that this may, in fact, be part of your journey to recovery. Always remember that no matter how many times you fall down, you need to pick yourself up and start again. Eventually, if you do not give up the good fight, you will succeed.

To everyone who suffers from addiction, I wish you success in your recovery, a long life, and much-deserved happiness. Mahalo!

Appendix

Other Resources:

Alcoholics Anonymous North Orange County
1111 East Commonwealth Ave., Suite D, Fullerton, CA 92831
(714) 773-4357 (24 hours) www.oc-aa.org

Al-Anon Orange County
(714) 748-1113
www.al-anon.alateen.org

Narcotics Anonymous Orange County
714.590-2388
http://www.orangecountyna.org/index.html

National Suicide Hotline (24 hours)
800-SUICIDE
800-784-2433
www.hopeline.com

Runaways—Counseling on many issues
800-843-5200
California Youth Crisis Line (24 hours)
California Coalition for Youth
www.calyouth.org

The Simple Screening Instrument for Substance Abuse (SSI-SA) was developed by the consensus panel of TIP 11, *Simple Screening Instruments for Outreach for Alcohol and Other Drug Abuse and Infectious Diseases* (Center for Substance Abuse Treatment 1994*c*).

With special thanks for all the research and materials funded, generated, and made available by the US Department of Health and Human Services
www.hhs.gov

Substance Abuse and Mental Health Services Administration
Center for Substance Abuse Treatment
www.samhsa.gov

National Institutes of Health
www.nih.gov

The National Institute on Drug Abuse
www.drugabuse.gov/publications/science-addiction

National Institute on Alcohol Abuse and Alcoholism
www.niaaa.nih.gov

References

ABC News. (2008). Heroin in Suburbia: New Face of Addiction. (Aug 04, 2008). Retrieved from: abcnews.go.com

Addiction Science Network A Primer on Drug Addiction. www. addictionscience.net/ASNreport01.htm. Retrieved From the Internet January 2012.

Alcoholics Anonymous, 4th edition. (2001). New York: Alcoholics Anonymous World Services, Inc.

American Psychiatric Association (APA). (2000). *Diagnostic and Statistical Manual of Mental Disorders. 4th ed. Text Revision. (DSM-IV-TR).* Washington, DC: American Psychiatric Association.

American Psychiatric Association. Practice Guideline for the Treatment of Patients with Substance Use Disorders. Arlington, VA: APA; 2007 Apr. Report No.: 164

Andrews, Paul W.; Thomson Jr., J. Anderson The bright side of being blue: Depression as an adaptation for analyzing complex problems. *Psychological Review,* Vol 116(3), Jul 2009, 620-654. doi: *10.1037/a0016242*

Arcelus J.; Vostanis P. (2005). Psychiatric comorbidity in children and adolescents. *Current Opinion in Psychiatry* 18(4):429-434.

Ausubel, D. P. (1980). An interactional approach to narcotic addiction. *National Institute on Drug Abuse (NIDA)*.

Research Monographs. Research Monograph Series 30, Selected Contemporary Theories, Library of Congress catalog card number 80-600058. DHHS publication number (ADM) 80-967.

Beck, A., Rush, A., Shaw, B. and Emery, G. (1979). Cognitive therapy of depression. New York: Guilford.

Beck, A., Wright, F., Newman, C. and Liese, B. (1993). Cognitive therapy of substance abuse. New York: Guilford.

Berberich, D. (1999), Attention deficit hyperactivity disorder: Differential diagnosis between hyperactive and inattentive type. (Doctoral dissertation). Fresno: CSPP.

Bokelmann, U. (International editor in chief). (April 2011). The First-Ever drug map of the body. *Ideas and Discoveries*.

Bozarth, M. (1994). Pleasure systems in the brain. In D. M. Warburton (ed.), *Pleasure: The politics and the reality* (pp. 5-14 + refs). New York: John Wiley & Sons. Retrieved from the Internet November 2011.

Bozarth, M. and Wise, R. (1985). Toxicity associated with long-term intravenous heroin and cocaine self-administration in the rat. *Journal of the American Medical Association*, 254, 81-83

Buddy T. (2006). Risk factors: Family history of alcoholism, disinhibition: Risks indicate probability, not certainty. Retrieved 2012: http://alcoholism.about.com/od/genetics/a/blacer060508.htm

Bullying and Suicide—Bullying Statistics. www.bullyingstatistics.org/content/bullying-and-suicide.html. Retrieved from Internet 2013.

Cyberbullying Research Summary. www.cyberbullying.us/cyberbullying_and_suicide. Retrieved from Internet 2013.

California Legislative Analyst Department. (2007). California's *Criminal Justice System: A Primer* www.lao.ca.gov. Retrieved from Internet 2012.

Cannon, W. (1929). Bodily changes in pain, hunger, fear, and rage. New York: Appleton-Century-Crofts.

Center for Substance Abuse Treatment. Addressing Co-Occurring Disorders in Non-Traditional Settings. COCE Overview Paper 4. Substance Abuse and Mental Health Services Administration. (2007).

Center for Substance Abuse Treatment. (1999). Enhancing motivation for change in substance abuse treatment. Treatment Improvement Protocol (TIP) Series Number 35, DHHS Pub. No. (SMA) 99-354. Rockville, MD: Substance Abuse and Mental Health Services Administration.

Center for Substance Abuse Treatment (1994). *TIP 11, Simple Screening Instruments for Outreach for Alcohol and Other Drug Abuse and Infectious Diseases.*

Christensen, C. (2006). Physiology of addiction. www.slideshare.net/jschwartz/physiology-of-addiction. Retrieved from Internet, 2011.

Council of Australian Governments (COAG). (2006). National Action Plan for Mental Health 2006-2011 (conference).

Crews, F. and Boettiger, C. (2009). Impulsivity, frontal lobes and risk for addiction. *Pharmacology, Biochemistry and Behavior*, 2009 September. 93(3): 237-247. doi: 10.1016/j.pbb.2009.04.018 Retrieved online 2012.

Chudler, Eric PhD. (2003) Neuroscience for Kids. What is Ecstasy (MDMA)? faculty.washington.edu/chudler/mdmah.html. Retrieved from the Internet 2012.

DiClemente, C., and Prochaska, J. (1982). Self change and therapy change of smoking behavior: A comparison of processes of change in cessation and maintenance. *Addictive Behavior.* 133-142.

Diener E., Lucas R., and Scollon C. Beyond the hedonic treadmill: revising the adaptation theory of well-being. *American Psychologist.* 2006 May-June; 61(4):305-14.

DuBois, S. (December 2008). Choosing Cocaine *Scienceline.* scienceline.org/2008/12/health-dubois-cocaine-rats-choice. Retrieved from the Internet 2012.

Elliott, Jeff (May 1993). "Just say nonsense—Nancy Reagan's drug education programs." *Washington Monthly*. p. 3. Retrieved from Internet 2012.

Giedd, J. (2011). Inside the teenage brain. Frontline. (Interview). http://www.pbs.org/wgbh/pages/frontline/shows/teenbrain/ interviews/giedd.html#ixzz1ZqcaOc3Y.

Hawking S., Mlodinow, L. (2010). The great design. New York: Bantam Books.

Health Resources and Services Administration (HRSA) Health disparities collaboratives: Models that are working mental health America. (2007). Conference: No Wrong Door—Integrated Mental Health and General Healthcare. Alexandria, Virginia. www.hrsa.gov/ index.html

Heinlein, R. (1961). Stranger in a strange land. New York, NY: G. P. Putnam's Sons. ISBN: 0808520873, 9780808520870.

Heron, M., Hoyert, D., Murphy S., Xu J., Kochanek K. and Tejada-Vera, B. (2006). Deaths: Final data for 2006. *National Vital Statistics Reports*; vol 57 no 14. Hyattsville, MD: National Center for Health Statistics. 2009, p. 11. http://www.cdc.gov/nchs/data/nvsr/nvsr57/nvsr57_14.pdf. Retrieved from the Internet January 2012.

Hettema, J., Steele. J., and Miller, W. (April 2005). *Annual Review of Clinical Psychology*, Vol.1:91-111.

Hopkins, J. and Sugerman, D. (1980) No one here gets out alive. Warner, Warner Books: NY.

Everitt, B., Belin D., Economidou, D., Pelloux Y., Dalley, J., and Robbins, T. (2008). Neural mechanisms underlying the vulnerability to develop compulsive drug-seeking habits and addiction. *Philosophical Transitions of the Royal Society B*. October 12; 363(1507): 3125-3135. doi: 10.1098/rstb.2008.0089

Frick, S. (2011). Heroin exacting a toll on suburbia (Oct 2011). Retrieved from: beaconnews.suntimes.com

Johns Hopkins Medicine Psychiatry and Behavioral Sciences, Mood Disorders Center. (Johns Hopkins 2012).
Adolescents at risk for familial bipolar disorder. Retrieved from the Internet 2012.
www.hopkinsmedicine.org/psychiatry/specialty_areas/moods/research/bioinformoodics.html.

Kabat-Zinn, J. (2010). Life is right now—Jon Kabat-Zinn on mindfulness. (Presentation). *You Tube.* Retrieved from Internet 2012.

Kabat-Zinn, J. (1990). Full catastrophe living. New York, NY: Bantam Dell.

Kabat-Zinn, J. (2005).Wherever you go there you are: Mindfulness meditation in everyday life, 10th anniversary edition. New York, NY: Hyperion.

Kalb, C. (September 27, 2004). Buddha Lessons. Newsweek. http://www.newsweek.com/2004/09/26/buddha-lessons.html. ©2011 The Newsweek/Daily Beast Company LLC. Retrieved from Internet 2012.

Koob, G., and Le Moa, l. (2005). Plasticity of reward neurocircuitry and the 'dark side' of drug addiction. *Nature Neuroscience.* Nov; 8 (11):1442-4. Molecular and Integrative Neurosciences Department, Scripps Research Institute, La Jolla, California, 92037, USA. gkoob@scripps.edu

McClellan, A., et al. (2000). Drug dependence, a chronic medical illness, implications for treatment, insurance, and outcome evaluation. *Journal of American Medical Association [JAMA]*, 284 (13): 1689-1695.

Miller, W. and Rollnick, S. (1991). Motivational interviewing: Preparing people for change. New York, NY: Guilford Press

Miller, W. and Rollnick, S. (2009). Ten things that motivational interviewing is not. *Behavioral and Cognitive Psychotherapy*, 37, 129-140.

Mitchell, A. and Lawrence, D. (2011). Revascularization and mortality rates following acute coronary syndromes in people with severe mental illness: comparative meta-analysis. *The British Journal of Psychiatry*, Vol. 198, 1.

Naar-King, S. and Suarez, M. (2011). Motivational interviewing with adolescents and young adults. NY, London: Guilford Press.

National Academy of Sciences. (2009). Preventing mental, emotional, and behavioral disorders among young people: Progress and possibilities.

National Adolescent Health Information Center. (2006). Fact sheet on suicide: Adolescents and young adults. San Francisco, CA: University of California, San Francisco.

National Center for Youth Law. (2003). www.youthlaw.org, revised. Retrieved from the Internet 2011.

National Center for Youth Law. (2007). *California Family Codes.* Retrieved from Internet 2011. www.youthlaw.org/fileadmin/teenhealth/teenhealthrights/ca/07_CA

National Institute on Drug Abuse, National Institute of Health, US Department of Health and Human Services. (August 2010). Drugs, brains, and behavior: The science of addiction.NIH Pub. No. 10-5605.

National Institute on Drug Abuse. (June 2008) NIDA notes: Vol. 21, No. 6. *Research Findings: New Therapy Reduces Drug Abuse Among Patients With Severe Mental Illness.* www.drugabuse.gov/NIDA_notes/NNvol21N6/new.html

National Institute on Drug Abuse (NIDA). National Institutes of Health, US Department of Health and Human Services. (2009). *Principles of Drug Addiction Treatment.* (2nd ed.) [Booklet].

National Institute on Drug Abuse (NIDA). (2009). *Treatment Approaches for Drug Addiction* (Revised). www.nida.nih.gov/Infofacts/TreatMeth.html

National Institute on Drug Abuse National Institutes of Health, US Department of Health and Human Services (2009). *Principles of Drug Addiction Treatment, a Research-Based Guide, 2nd Edition.*

National Institute of Health (NIH) and the National Institute on Drug Abuse (2004). Co-Occurring Disorders Increase Suicide Risk, Early Drug Use a Factor in Adolescents. Retrieved from Internet 2012.

National Institute of Mental Health (NIMH). (2007). www.nimh.nih.
gov/health/publications/suicide.
Retrieved from Internet 2011.

National Survey on Drug Use and Health. (May 2005). The NSDUH
Report: First Use of Marijuana: Average Annual Rates. www.samhsa.
gov/data/marijuana.htm Retrieved from Internet 2012

Neuroanatomy and Physiology of Brain Reward II. ibgwww.colorado.
edu/cadd/a_drug/essays/essay4.htm.
Retrieved from Internet 2013.

O'Connell, E., Ellen, M. and Boat, T. *(Editor)*. (2009). Preventing
mental, emotional, and behavioral disorders among young people:
Progress and possibilities. Committee on the prevention of mental
disorders and substance abuse among children, youth and young,
Institute of Medicine, National Research Council, National
Academies Press.

Office of Juvenile Justice and Delinquency Prevention (OJJDP). (2009).
Statistical briefing book.
www.ojjdp.gov/ojstatbb/crime. Retrieved from Internet 2011.

Orange County Health Care Agency, Orange County, California (July
2009). *Self-Inflicted Injury & Suicide in Orange County-Based on 2005-2007
Emergency Department, Hospitalization and Death Records*

Pharmacology Biochemical Behaviorism. (2009) September; 93(3):
237-247. Published online May 3, 2009.
Retrieved from Internet 2012.

Potenza, M. N. and Taylor, J. R. (2009). Found in translation:
Understanding impulsivity and related constructs through integrative
preclinical and clinical research. *Biological Psychiatry*. 2009 October 15;
66(8): 714-716. doi:10.1016/j.biopsych.2009.08.004 Retrieved 2012
from: ww.ncbi.nlm.nih.gov/pmc/articles/PMC2801557.

Prochaska, J. O. and DiClemente, C. C. (1982). Transtheoretical
therapy: Toward a more integrative model of change.
Psychotherapy: theory, research and practice, 19: 276-288.

Queensland Divisions of General Practice policy (QLD). 2008.
www.health.qld.gov.au/.../annualreport2008/docs/QH_section-4.pdf

Ramo, D., Brown, Sandra A. (Sep. 2008). Classes of substance abuse
relapse situations: A comparison of adolescents and adults. *Psychology
of Addictive Behaviors*, Vol 22(3), Sep 2008, 372-379. doi: 10.1037/0893-
164X.22.3.372. Retrieved from the Internet 2012.

Robinson, T. E. (1993). The neural basis of drug craving: an
incentive-sensitization theory of addiction. *Brain Research. Brain Research
Review. Sep-Dec;18 (3):247-91.* Department of Psychology, Univ. of
Michigan.

Rogers, Carl (1951). Client-centered therapy. Cambridge
Massachusetts: The Riverside Press.

Rosenzweig, M., Leiman, A., and Breedlove, S. M. (1996). Biological
psychology. Massachusetts: Sinauer Associates.

Sabatinelli, D., Lang, P. J., Bradley, M. M., Costa, V. D., and Versace,
F. (2007). Pleasure rather than salience activates human nucleus
accumbens and medial prefrontal cortex. Journal of Neurophysiology
98 (9): 1374-1379. doi:10.1152/jn.00230.2007. PMID 17596422.

Sarver, S. (March/April 2007). Bully-Busting Basics. *Unique
Opportunities, the Physician's Resource.*

Segal, Z., J., Williams, M. J., Teasdale, J. (2002). *Mindfulness-Based
Cognitive Therapy for Depression: A New Approach to Preventing Relapse.* New
York, NY: Guilford Press.

Seligman, M. (2003). Authentic happiness. Great Britain: Nicholas
Brealey Publishing

Seligman, Martin. (1993). What you can change and what you can't.
Columbine, NY: Fawcett

Seligman, M., Reivich, K., Jaycock, L., and Gillham, J. (1995). The
optimistic child: How learned optimism protects children from
depression. New York: Houghton Mifflin Company.

Smith, D., Boel-Studt, S., Cleeland, L. (2009).Parental consent in adolescent substance abuse treatment outcome studies. *Journal of Substance Abuse Treatment.*

Spatz-Widom, C., Hiller-Sturmhöfel, S. (2005). Alcohol abuse as a risk factor for and consequence of child abuse. pubs.niaaa.nih.gov/publications/arh25-1/52-57.htm. Retrieved from Internet 2011.

Substance Abuse and Mental Health Services Administration Center for Substance Abuse Treatment (SAMHSA) www.samhsa.gov. Retrieved 2011

Substance Abuse and Mental Health Services Administration [SAMHSA]. (2009). Rockville, MD: Center for Mental Health Services, Substance Abuse and Mental Health Services Administration, US Department of Health and Human Services. Integrated Treatment for Co-Occurring Disorders: Evidence-based practices KIT. DHHS Pub. No. SMA-08-4366.

Substance Abuse and Mental Health Services Administration (SAMHSA) (Reprinted 2011). Center for Substance Abuse Treatment. Substance Abuse Treatment for Person's with Co-Occurring Disorders. Treatment Improvement Protocol (TIP) Series, No. 42.

Substance Abuse and Mental Health Services Administration (SAMHSA). (2007). Center for Mental Health Services; Center for Substance Abuse Treatment*Understanding Evidence-Based Practices for Co-Occurring Disorders,* COCE Overview Paper 5.DHHS Publication No. (SMA) 07-4278. Rockville, MD.

Surgeon General's Conference on Children's Mental Health (2000). A National Action Agenda. September 18-19, 2000. www.surgeongeneral. gov/topics/cmh/childreport.html. Retrieved from Internet 2012.

Szasz, T. (1960). The Myth of mental illness. American Psychologist, 15, 113-118. Retrieved 2012 from psychclassics.yorku.ca/Szasz/myth.htm. ISSN 1492-3713. Originally Posted January 2002.

Substance Abuse and Mental Health Services Administration (SAMHSA). (2010). *Results from the 2010 National Survey on Drug Use and Health: Summary of National Findings,* NSDUH Series H-41, HHS Publication No. (SMA) 11-4658. Rockville, MD: Substance Abuse and Mental Health Services Administration, 2011.

Trujillo, K. A. and Molina, P. (2007). Effects of drugs of use on the brain and on adolescent brain development, In: Drug Abuse among Hispanics: A Brief Evidence-Based Guide for Providers, SAMHSA. Retrieved online:
http://store.samhsa.gov/shin/content//SMA07-4288/SMA07-4288.pdf

Trujillo, K. A. (2002). The neurobiology of opiate tolerance, dependence and sensitization: mechanisms of NMDA receptor dependent synaptic plasticity. *Neurotoxicity Research,* 4(4), 373-391.

United States Census Bureau (2010). *Census Bureau Homepage.* www.census.gov

United States Department of Veteran Affairs, 2010. *www.mentalhealth.va.gov.* Retrieved from Internet 2012.

United States Department of Health and Human Services, Substance Abuse and Mental Health Services Administration Center for Substance Abuse Treatment. *Quick Guide for Mental Health Professionals,* TIP 42. 2005.

United States Department of Justice, National Drug Intelligence Center. (February 2010). *National Drug Threat Assessment 2010.* www.gov/ndic/pubs38/38661/drugImpact.htm. Retrieved from the Internet 2012.

Vaillant. G. (1995). The Natural history of alcoholism revisited. Cambridge, Massachusetts: Harvard University Press.

Walter Bradford Cannon (1929). Bodily changes in pain, hunger, fear, and rage. New York: Appleton-Century-Crofts.

Wikipedia. (2012). wikipedia.org/wiki/Seize_the_moment. Retrieved from Internet March 13, 2012.

Williams, M., Teasdale, J., Zindel, S. and Kabat-Zinn, J. (2007). The mindful way through depression: Freeing yourself from chronic unhappiness. New York, NY: Guilford Press.

Yalom, I. (1995). The theory and practice of group psychotherapy 4th edition. New York, NY: Basic Books.

Index

8884059R00098

Made in the USA
San Bernardino, CA
25 February 2014